CHRIST'S WAY
OF MAKING DISCIPLES

PHILIP G. SAMAAN

Books by Philip G. Samaan

E-mail: pgs@southern.edu

CHRIST'S WAY
OF MAKING DISCIPLES

PHILIP G. SAMAAN

COLLEGE PRESS

Unless otherwise noted, the Bible citations are from the New King James
Version. Copyright© 1979, 1980, 1982, Thomas Nelson, Inc., Publishers.

Texts credited to the NEB are from *The New English Bible.*© The Delegates of the Oxford University Press and the Syndics of the Cambridge University Press 1961, 1970. Reprinted by permission.

Bible texts credited to Phillips are from]. B. Phillips: *The New Testament in Modem English*, Revised Edition. © J. B. Phillips 1958, 1960, 1972. Used by permission of Macmillan Publishing Co.

Texts credited to RSV are from the Revised Standard Version of the Bible, copyright © 1946, 1959, 1971 by the Division of Christian Education of the National Council of the Churches of Christ in the U.S.A. Used by permission.

This book was
Edited by Richard W. Coffen
Copy edited by William Cleveland and James Cavil
Cover designed by Megan Keller
Cover illustration by Del Parson
Typeset: 12/15 Bembo

PRINTED IN U.S.A.

08 07 06 05   6 5 4 3

248.4

ISBN 0-8280-1417-5

Printed by Review and Herald® Publishing Association

Reprinted by College Press Publishing LLC

Dedication

Dedicated
to Jesus Christ
the Supreme Disciple-maker

Contents

Introduction

Ever since the publication of my book *Christ's Way of Reaching People*, I have sensed the need to follow it up with works on Christ's way to spirituality and disciple-making. By the grace of God the sequel, *Christ's Way to Spiritual Growth*, was published, and again by His grace I am commencing yet another sequel, *Christ's Way of Making Disciples*. The work on spirituality was indeed imperative in the series, for it is the bedrock of witnessing, disciple-making, and any other service in Christ's cause. Our duty to Christ must always issue from our devotion to Christ.

The title of each book begins with the words "Christ's way" in order to focus our attention on the Master Himself rather than on any other method, individual, or institution. He alone can show us the way to "grow up in all things into Him who is the head" (Eph. 4:15). After all, Christ Himself is *the* Way to all and any effectual ministry. He is indeed "the way, the truth, and the life" (John 14:6), and those who walk in Him are faithful followers of "the Way" (Acts 9:2).

The purpose of the first book in the series, *Christ's Way of Reaching People,* was to present a basic course in witnessing. It presented six steps: Jesus' mingling with others as one who (1) desired their good, (2) sympathized with them, (3) ministered to their needs, (4) won their trust, (5) bade them to follow Him, and (6) made them fishers of men. This present work builds on the earlier book and launches out from its last step of making "fishers of men" toward becoming disciples and disciplers of others.

Witnessing and disciple-making must always remain linked together. Adding new converts must be followed up with multiplying fruit-bearing disciples. "Just as evangelism is analogous to putting plants out in a garden," explains Carl Wilson, "so disciple building is analogous to tending a garden" *(With Christ in the School of Disciple Building,* p. 211).

Therefore, let us not limit our ministry to merely winning souls, but let us press on to the fullness of Christ's vision in His school of disciple-making. Let us focus our minds on Christ's effective way of reproducing and multiplying disciples who, in their turn, reproduce and multiply themselves through others, thus building up His body in the world.

May this earnest effort to engage us more fully in Christ's way facilitate us to become His type of fruitful disciples and disciple-makers. May this dynamic process of disciple-making permeate our being so that it will not be exhausting overwork, but exhilarating overflow of His ministry through our ministry. May His mission never stagnate, but overflow through the open channels of our lives, producing an abundant harvest of disciples and disciple-makers for advancing His kingdom. As devoted disciples, let us wholeheartedly heed our Master's mandate to make disciples of all nations until His glorious appearing.

CHAPTER ONE

The MISSION of Making Disciples

Imagine taking a guided tour of an enormous light bulb factory that has been operating for many years. During the tour the production manager mentions the huge efforts and large sums of money invested in building up the plant to its full efficiency. The employees are paid decent wages, all the sophisticated machinery is in place, and the resource materials to produce light bulbs are available in abundant supply. And throughout the excursion we find ourselves extremely impressed with all the hustle and bustle of the various activities.

Rounding the last corner in the factory and having seen all that we possibly could see, we turn instinctively to the manager and ask him to show us some of his fine light bulbs. He seems to be caught off guard and unprepared for this inquiry, so we ask tactfully, "How many light bulbs does your factory produce in a day?"

Baffled by our intrusive question, he responds curtly, "None."

"But how many bulbs do you make in a week, in a month, in a year?" we persist.

Irritated now, he blurts out, "None whatsoever! But

you need to understand, however, that we have been extremely busy running the plant."

EFFICIENCY AND EFFECTIVENESS

We can hardly conceive of such an unlikely scenario in the real world of production and business. Obviously the sole purpose for the existence of a light bulb plant is to produce light bulbs. If not, either radical changes would have to take place, or such an unproductive operation would quickly be forced out of business. Yet unfortunately this happens all too often in the church—God's plant to produce His spiritual light bulbs in this dark world.

We seem to be *efficient* in the business of maintaining, running, and even adding new members to the church, but hardly *effective* in the ministry of growing fruitful disciples. Let us suppose that we call on several churches in our area to find out how many disciple-makers they have produced. We explain that we need such disciplers to help us equip new converts in the work of ministry. Such an inquiry is quite legitimate, because disciplers are the greatest spiritual product reproduced by Christ in His church.

What do you suppose the response would be? Would it be, for instance, "We have many people attending our services" or "Let me send you some information about the various activities we sponsor"? Would our question sound strange? But why would it if the church exists to produce disciple-makers? And would it surprise us if such a rare product exists—the precious product of a disciple-maker who knows how to disciple someone from conversion all the way to fruit-bearing discipleship? In time such a fruit-bearing disciple could reproduce that process in another person.

Regrettably, too many church members, as well as their pastors, are neither engaged in growing disciples nor seriously planning on it. Even more regrettable is that all too often they do not perceive such a situation to be an apparent aberration in the Christian life. George Orwell aptly wrote: "We have now sunk to a depth at which the restatement of the obvious is the first duty of intelligent men" (in Bill Hull, *The Disciple-making Pastor,* p. 13). We get bogged down by anything and everything about the business of the church except the one indispensable thing—making fruitful disciples.

Somehow in a maze of many distractions and complexities, common sense becomes very uncommon. The commonsensical thing of producing such disciplers becomes uncommon and deplorably neglected. But that is precisely the church's reason for being. *"The crisis at the heart of the church is a crisis of product,"* Bill Hull asserts. That precious product was clearly commanded by Christ: make disciples. And Christ's genius of a strategy "makes so much sense," Hull continues, "because disciples penetrate their world. Disciples reproduce themselves, which leads to multiplication. Multiplication is the key to reaching the world and fulfilling the Great Commission" *(ibid.,* pp. 14, 15).

Christ's Passion and Priority

Yes, making disciples was the prevailing passion and top priority of Christ in order to proliferate His gospel, and that must be our passion and priority as well. The Gospels are replete with ample evidence that disciple-making was Christ's supreme strategy for propagating His message to the ends of the earth. And aptly, at the culmination of His earthly ministry of training His disciples, His parting words to them breathed disciple-making: "Go therefore and *make disciples* of all the nations" (Matt. 28:19).

"It is finished" (John 19:30) is what Jesus uttered to His Father and the universe as He breathed His last on the cross. Then what did He mean earlier in John 17:4 when He confirmed to His Father that His assigned work was finished? "I have glorified You on the earth," He prayed. "I have finished the work which You have given Me to do." This declaration was made in the context of His high-priestly prayer in behalf of His disciples. He must have been referring to them, for He mentioned them 40 times in the course of the prayer. He glorified His Father in the training of His disciples.

"Christ had finished the work that was given Him to do. He had gathered out those who were to continue His work among men. And He said, 'I am glorified in them' " (Ellen G. White, *The Acts of the Apostles,* p. 24).

Of course, what He had accomplished on the cross was the ultimate giving of His life for the redemption of millions. But His work of giving of Himself to the disciples for discipleship was vital. Through them He intended to greatly reproduce and multiply Himself and His message of redemption to the world. He touched the lives of many, but in a special way He invested Himself to train those 12 men. Hence He bequeathed His legacy not just to anyone, but to the few whom He had fully trained to reflect His image and reproduce His ministry in the lives of many. Besides His completed and indispensable work on the cross, those disciples were also His work that He came to accomplish.

HIS MISSION, THEIR MISSION

On the day of His resurrection Jesus said to His disciples: "Peace to you! As the Father has sent Me, I also send you" (John 20:21). In going back to heaven, He transferred His Father's mission to them. His mission was to become their mission, and it was to be carried out in the same manner as He Himself carried it out. In entrusting them with it, He confirmed that they were now ready—trained, equipped, and deployable.

The disciples did not become demoralized because of His departure, but rather became more determined than ever to disciple others. They did not request another discipler, because now, under the guidance of the Holy Spirit, they themselves were disciplers. These men did not regress to fishing, but progressed to fulfill their Master's Great Commission. Fashioned by Him and empowered by His Spirit, they made His Great Commission their grand mission, infiltrating the known world and making disciples of others as Christ made disciples of them.

Caught up in this momentous mission, they were propelled by the power of His divine authority and energized by the promise of His everlasting presence. Directly preceding and following His mandate in Matthew 28:19, He spoke assurance to them: "All authority has been given to Me in heaven and on earth" (verse 18). And "I am with you always, even to the end of the age" (verse 20). They keenly sensed in a brand-new way that the King of the universe was now deploying them to share His life and ministry in the world. They knew better now than ever before that with all His authority, power, and presence they would indeed make and multiply disciples, conquering the world for His glory.

Growing disciples is equivalent to making followers, learners, emulators of Christ. Such discipling is intertwined with personal affection and adherence to the Master Discipler Himself, whereby His life and mission become reproduced in the discipled. "Christ did not fail, neither was He discouraged; and the disciples were to show a faith of the *same* enduring nature. They were to work *as* He had worked, depending on Him for strength. Though their way would be obstructed by apparent impossibilities, yet by His grace they were to go forward, *despairing of nothing and hoping for everything*" (*The Acts of the Apostles,* p. 23; italics supplied).

The pertinent principle here is that we disciple others the way we have been discipled ourselves. And we reproduce in others what has been reproduced in us—the glorious fruit of walking and working with Jesus. Therefore, our mission as disciplers, in Juan Ortiz' unmistakable words, is "to make disciples who make disciples who make disciples who make disciples" (*Call to Discipleship,* p. 18).

Thus the whole web of humanity becomes infected with the contagious results of following Christ's way and obeying His commission of making disciples. This precise and clear charter to His disciples, the executors of His last will and testament, seems "so unassuming in its simplicity, yet invincible in its ultimate triumph," writes Robert Coleman. "Just as they had been discipled, so they were to disciple others, teaching them in turn to do the same, until through this process of multiplication, their witness reached the uttermost parts of the world" (*The Mind of the Master,* p. 8).

THE BEDROCK AND THE BUILDER

This "gospel commission is the great missionary *charter* of Christ's kingdom" *(The Acts of the Apostles,* p. 28; italics supplied). It is the divine document that sets forth the principles and practices of finishing our Lord's work prior to His second coming. Jesus, the ingenious Architect of this charter, spent three and a half years carefully constructing the firm foundation of the edifice of His mission. He, the Master Builder, constructed its foundation from the 12 disciples, who were supported by Him, the eternal Bedrock holding up that foundation.

He is indeed the Builder as well as the Bedrock. Paul declares that "no other foundation can anyone lay than that which is Jesus Christ" (1 Cor. 3:11) and that we are "built on the foundation of the apostles and prophets" (Eph. 2:20). In the construction of the edifice of His mission, much would depend on the quality training of the 12 disciples whom He had chosen. That was it. He had no other plan to continue the work He had started of multiplying the making of disciples. Sublime yet simple strategy.

In such a strategy, Jesus bypassed the self-righteous and educated Jewish teachers, but He chose teachable, simple, and unlearned men to move the entire world. "These men He purposed to *train* and *educate* as the *leaders* of His church. They *in turn* were to *educate others and send them out* with the gospel message." Thus "by these feeble agencies, through His word and Spirit, He designs to place salvation within the reach of all" *(The Acts of the Apostles,* pp. 17, 18; italics supplied).

SUBLIME YET SIMPLE STRATEGY

This simple yet invincible plan really works, and this is

how: the disciplers in the body of Christ disciple other members to be disciplers, educating and engaging them in works of service, and so on in an unending cycle of re-production and multiplication. Through the gifts of the Holy Spirit, Christ has given to His church discipling lead-ers such as apostles, prophets, evangelists, pastor-teachers "for the equipping of the saints for the work of ministry" (Eph. 4:11, 12).

That is it! The church's charter—its mandate, its mis-sion, and its reason for being—educate others to educate; train others to train; disciple others to disciple. "The church of Christ is organized for *service*. Its watchword is *ministry*. Its members are soldiers, to be *trained* for conflict under the Captain of their salvation. Christian ministers, physicians, teachers, have a *broader* work than many have recognized. They are *not only* to minister to the people, but to *teach them to minister*. They should *not only* give in-struction in the right principles, but *educate* their hearers to *impart* these principles." Indeed, "*every church* should be a *training school* for Christian workers" (Ellen G. White, *The Ministry of Healing,* pp. 148, 149; italics supplied).

A PREVAILING PRIORITY

This must be the pastor's explicit and prevailing prior-ity, the one attraction among the many competing distrac-tions pastors encounter daily. Everything is determined by heeding or unheeding this mandate of Christ for propagat-ing His ministry. This proliferating process in the church must start with at least one person, and hopefully that will be the pastor or the spiritual leader. Obviously, such a per-son must himself or herself be discipled to disciple others.

Christ must reproduce Himself and His ministry in them so that they in turn reproduce such in the lives of their spiritual apprentices.

An old pastor shared with me his experience of spending many years of his ministry distracted by a myriad of chores in running the church. He confided that throughout his ministry he felt more or less like a failure, that something was missing. With a gleam in his eyes, he said that a few years before his retirement his ministry was radically rejuvenated. What happened? He had heard a Christian discipler speak on the priority of sharing Christ's mandate of making disciples. Why had he not seen this long before then? he wondered.

He went back to his church, determined to do something about it. He remembered the speaker stating that the mandate was simple and sensible in its method, yet supernatural in its outcome. And he started out simple, trusting the outcome to God. The Holy Spirit impressed him to disciple one member, sharing his life and ministry with him. That discipled member became a discipler of another member, and that of another and another. And within three years this discipling ministry was reproduced and multiplied many times over, infecting his whole congregation.

The pastor was now surrounded by a detachment of dedicated and deployable disciplers, devoted to Christ and determined to reproduce His ministry in others. More thrilling to the old pastor was that this ever-expanding spiritual brigade continued in ministry and disciple-making even after he retired and moved on. He testified that those few years were the best of his entire ministry and that he wished such had been the case in his ministry from the very beginning.

The genius of this plan is indeed far-reaching and rev-olutionary. For in such a process of growing disciples, spir-itually healthy disciples and disciplers are reproduced, who in turn reproduce and multiply after their kind. Thus spir-itual health and vitality pervade the body of Christ, making it grow and multiply in its impact on the world around it.

This is the mission of making disciples. In the rest of this book we will focus on the different aspects of how Christ went about accomplishing such a mission. He is indeed the Master of the mission, as we shall see in the next chapter.

CHAPTER TWO

The MASTER
of the Mission

Needing to get away from the pressures of school, a group of us college students had organized a weekend retreat at a lodge in a secluded wooded area near the Oregon coast. Coming to the end of a hectic week of study and work, I remember us finding ourselves frantically preparing for this event. In the rush to make arrangements for our food, transportation, and weekend activities, we overlooked getting adequate directions to the lodge. For some reason no one emerged as the group leader, nor was anyone assigned to be one. And whenever I inquired as to how to get there, nobody seemed to have a clear idea. Repeatedly I would hear, "Don't worry; we'll get there . . . somehow." I have never liked to live with much ambiguity anyway, and this time was no exception.

The plan was to park our cars along the side of the highway and then walk the rest of the way to the lodge. Having started our trip late that Friday afternoon, we did not arrive until night. It was pouring rain, dark, and cold; and for lack of a better idea, we carried our provisions and headed aimlessly into the dark woods. Wouldn't you know it? We spent almost the entire night totally lost, heading in all directions on muddy trails and going in circles that led nowhere. Oh, how *desperately* we felt the need for a *leader* who knew the way! A leader to provide the needed guidance in such chaos for a bunch of lost, exhausted, hungry, and miserable students.

THE NEED FOR A LEADER

Without a guide a retreat can turn into chaos, and without a commander no battle plan can succeed. Likewise, the mission of making disciples ends up in shambles without the Master. We march under His guidance in this momentous mission. He knows the way, for He *is* the Way. We fear no darkness, for He is the light of the world. And when we become weak and exhausted, He is our strength and sustenance. None of us can be a match for such a momentous mission without Christ our Master. If we think otherwise, we become conceited and discouraged. It is true that we are servants best when we put the Saviour first.

A creative and energetic pastor told me of the crushing burden and disappointment he experienced in trying to engage his church in a discipling program. He did not seem to know it at the time, but later he realized that he had been acting as if *he* were the master of the mission. He felt as though the burden of the lost world was upon *his* shoulders. We must never forget that it is the *Lord's* work, the *Lord's* mission. It is the Lord's battle, not ours.

That is precisely what His Word says: "The battle is the Lord's" (1 Sam. 17:47) and "The battle is not yours, but God's" (2 Chron. 20:15). He launches it; He fights and sustains it. And He wins it decisively. He is our

Commander-in-chief, and we are His loyal soldiers, fully engaged under the able command of One who has never lost a single battle, nor will He ever. He came here to win, and He did decisively.

AN ABLE COMMANDER

Temporal plans to conquer the world impose change from the outside in. But His battle plan for spiritual world conquest is to mold the lives of people—originally 12 of them—from the inside out into His likeness. And that nucleus of the Twelve was to reproduce and multiply until the entire world would be captured for Christ.

Here's how Robert Coleman describes this failproof plan: "Like a general plotting His course of battle, the Son of God calculated to win. He could not afford to take a chance. Weighing every alternative and variable factor in human experience, He conceived a plan that would not fail" *(The Master Plan of Evangelism,* p. 18).

A MASTER ARCHITECT AND BUILDER

Two powerful New Testament analogies show clearly how Christ is portrayed as the Master in building up His kingdom through His disciples. The first analogy describes Him as the Master Builder and the Chief Cornerstone of His spiritual edifice. The second one represents Him as the Head, guiding in the building up of His body, the church.

Like jagged stones hewed from the quarry of life, we submit ourselves to the Master's skilled hands to be chiseled and polished into a shape fit for His temple. The living Chief Cornerstone loves to mold and multiply us into living stones so that He may build us up into His spiritual edifice to advance His kingdom. Peter depicts Christ as a "living stone" (1 Peter 2:4), and he applies the same term to us: "You also, as living stones, are being built up a spiritual house, a holy priesthood" (verse 5). This shows that, as our Chief, Jesus intimately identifies with us in the building up of His kingdom. He is God, but with us. We become living stones only in our living connection with the living Christ, only as we submit ourselves to Him so that He can reproduce Himself in us.

No, we do not build up ourselves, because the chiseling as well as the building belongs to Christ, the Master Builder. Notice that He is the active agent and we are the recipients: We "are being built up" (verse 5), and also we "are being built together" (Eph. 2:22). But He is not only the Builder of this spiritual edifice; He is the Architect of its blueprint and the Bedrock of its foundation.

Furthermore, He is the "chief cornerstone, in whom the whole building, being joined together, grows into a holy temple in the Lord, in whom you also are being built together for a habitation of God in the Spirit" (verses 20-22). Yes, He is a "living stone," but He is also the "chief cornerstone," which "lines up the foundation and the superstructure and binds the walls together" *(The Seventh-day Adventist Bible Commentary,* vol. 7, pp. 560, 561). As the Master in the building up and multiplying of the members of His body, He is the Initiator, the Sustainer, and the Finisher of such a spiritual edifice. What better position can we possibly find ourselves in than to be the living stones in the Master's glorious building project?

Building up such living stones into His spiritual house is parallel to building up His disciples as living members in

His body. The spiritual building up of His body occurs when we avail ourselves of Christ's leadership to equip us in the ministry of disciple-making. That we may "grow up in all things into Him who is head—Christ—from whom the whole body, joined and knit together by what every joint supplies, according to the effective working by which every part does its share, causes growth of the body for the edifying of itself in love" (Eph. 4:15, 16).

THE HEAD AND THE HEART OF THE MISSION

If we use the illustration that Christ's mission of growing disciples is the cardiovascular system of His body, then He, the Master of such mission, is its central nervous system. The head and the heart are indispensable to each other and to the rest of the body for preserving its life and promoting its health and growth. The heart, the blood vessels, and the blood they pump and circulate all make up the cardiovascular system. The life-giving blood is pumped by the heart through the blood vessels to the remotest parts of the body, thus supplying the cells with nourishment essential for their growth and multiplication in the building up of the body. Blood is indispensable to every part of the body. If its supply is contaminated and its circulation is poor, then the whole body suffers and deteriorates.

Bill Hull attributes the deterioration in the church to a heart crisis in the body of Christ. "The church's cardiovascular system, its most crucial part, determines the health of the entire body," he writes. And "like any crisis of the cardiovascular system, this has left the church weak and dependent" *(The Disciple Making Pastor,* pp. 12, 14).

What has plunged the church into such a critical crisis?

The diagnosis reveals its dismal failure to make and reproduce fruit-bearing disciples who will penetrate and impact the world. When the church's cardiovascular system "produces and reproduces the right product, like any healthy body, it will be able to carry out its function. When we obey Christ's commission, two good things happen: we create healthy Christians; healthy Christians reproduce, and the body grows, then multiplies, and the world become evangelized" *(ibid., pp. 14, 15)*.

That is what happens when we obey our Master's Great Commission to make disciples. But if we, the cardiovascular system of the body—to stay with our analogy—disobey the command of the Head to make disciples, then atrophy sets in. The Head must always coordinate, control, and command the whole body in all its functions in order for it to develop and be strong. Likewise, unless Christ is always Lord of all in our lives, He is not Lord at all.

Christ our Master is the head, or the brain, of His mission of making disciples. The brain, the master control center of the body, works through the nervous system. It is one of the most amazing designs in God's creation. It is the most highly organized unit of any form of life, and functions as a superefficient command post, communicating, coordinating, and controlling all bodily activities.

MOLDED BY THE MASTER

"As the tree strikes its roots down into the soil for nourishment and moisture, so the growing child of God reaches up to Christ for his vitality and sustenance. Union with Christ is at once the cause and the result of growth.

He is the head of each man as well as head of the church." Furthermore, "growing up into Him assures vitality flowing from Him into the members of the body, which are closely joined together" *(The SDA Bible Commentary,* vol. 6, p. 1025).

As we grow up into Christ, the Head, He reproduces His likeness in our lives, then He helps us reproduce such likeness in the lives of others. He wants us to consider Him as the perfect pattern for everything that has to do with disciple-making. This mission is centered in His person, and its mandate and reproduction are bound up in His life. The heart of His plan is that "He does not ask us to follow a theory, but to follow a Person," Robert Coleman asserts. "His life is the illustration of what He wants His disciples to become" *(The Master Plan of Evangelism,* p. 13).

"A disciple is not above his teacher," Jesus said, "but everyone who is perfectly trained will become like his teacher" (Luke 6:40).

First, true disciples are submissive and receptive to the Master—submissive to His leadership and receptive to His instructions. There is no formation without submission and reception. "The great Master Worker desires to mold and fashion us." Yes, He is fully committed to this task; but "we are not to try to do the work of the potter. Our part is to yield ourselves to be molded by the Master Worker" (Ellen G. White, *The Ministry of Healing,* p. 472).

Second, there is a need for training, full training, by the Master. He does not command us to make disciples before blazing the trail for us to follow. He commissions us to do what He has already done—in our lives. Michael Griffiths observes that Jesus did not merely command His disciples, but prior to that, "his own life and ministry provided them with a pattern and prototype for all subsequent missionary endeavor" *(The Example of Jesus,* p. 155).

Third, such devotion to and training by the Master results in the disciples becoming like their Master. Christ can use us to fashion others in His image only if we ourselves are fashioned in that image. This calls for spiritual growth and maturity. We just cannot go on staggering and stagnating in our spiritual infancy, but we must go on to maturity, attaining to "the measure of the stature of the fullness of Christ" and thus "may grow up in all things into Him who is the Head—Christ" (Eph. 4:13-15).

This is indeed the greatest spiritual product the Master Teacher and Trainer can produce in the members of His body, the church. These faithful and fruitful disciples live His life and do His work. Throughout His ministry Christ's relentless effort was to train fully His disciples to make disciples. He masterfully executed a powerful plan to reproduce progressively His life and perpetuate His labor in them.

Of course, Christ wants us to become His devoted disciples. However, notice that in His Great Commission He does not call us to merely *enjoy* being disciples, but to *engage* ourselves in making disciples (Matt. 28:19). As devoted disciples we must develop into determined disciplers in order to align ourselves with His grand strategy of multiplying His ministry worldwide. Discipleship was never primarily intended to benefit the disciples, but to bless all humanity. "To stop short of that," writes LeRoy Eims, "is to fail to capture the genius of the commission of Christ" *(The Lost Art of Disciple Making,* p. 83).

The Discipled Become Disciplers

The Master's foremost priority is to produce and perpetuate His life and message of salvation through us. And through such reproduction multiplication results, and the new disciples themselves take their turn in becoming disciplers. Thus qualitatively and quantitatively Christ's powerful plan of global evangelism leads to an ever-widening circle of spiritual reproduction and multiplication of the best and most fruitful disciples.

Many of us are all too ready to boast with the success of adding new members to the church, but we are painfully quiet when too many of the new members shirk their responsibility to become disciplers themselves. Following the Master's plan of making disciples will help extricate us from this dire dilemma. It will disciple the new members and make them disciplers of others as well. And happily, in this process they themselves continue to thrive spiritually, while at the same time they reproduce and multiply themselves in others—a multiplication of spiritual blessings indeed!

Implicit Trust in the Master

If we keep uppermost in our minds that Christ is the only Master of the mission of disciple-making, we will not become demoralized and dependent upon human masters and institutions. Ellen White cautions: "In our work for God there is danger of relying too largely upon what man with his talents and ability can do. Thus we lose sight of the one Master Worker. . . . It is a great mistake to trust in human wisdom or numbers in the work of God. Successful work for Christ depends not so much on numbers or talent as upon pureness of purpose, the true simplicity of earnest, dependent faith" *(The Desire of Ages,* p. 370).

This is precisely the urgent need of the church today: trusting implicitly in the Master of the mission to empower us so that we can help multiply fruit-bearing disciples and not merely adding new members. Christ's mission for us is not to baby-sit spiritual infants and hover over weak church members. It is to grow them into strong fruitful disciples who will reach to the other members of the body.

This is unequivocally Christ's vital vision and momentous mission for us. He connects discipleship with abundant fruit-bearing. A devoted disciple who abides in Christ "bears much fruit" (John 15:5). Moreover, He declares that "by this My Father is glorified, that you bear much fruit; so you will be My disciples" (verse 8). It is His mission. He initiated it, modeled it, and completed it. And now He wants you and me to implement it in His name, under His authority, and with His presence, until He comes.

He wants us to be indelibly branded with the mark of the mission.

CHAPTER THREE

The MARK
of the Mission

An eloquent actor was once asked to recite publicly the twenty-third psalm. He did so with great effectiveness. His diction and articulation were impeccable; his inflection and tempo were compelling. At the end his hearers were so impressed that they gave him a standing ovation.

When things calmed down, the actor, having spotted an old preacher in the audience, called him to the stage and asked him if he would repeat the same psalm. The preacher acquiesced, and at the close of his presentation there was total silence. The audience was engrossed in thoughtful contemplation, gripped to the core by the presentation, and hardly any eyes remained dry.

Standing beside this old preacher, the actor put his arm around him as he addressed the attentive assembly: "Ladies and gentlemen, we both repeated the same psalm, but obviously there was a difference. The difference is this: I know the psalm, but this man knows the Shepherd."

THE TRADEMARK OF THE MASTER TEACHER

This is the most unmistakable mark of the Master's mission of growing disciples: to know the Shepherd and to be like Him. Just as a trademark distinguishes the product of a company, so Christ's product of a disciple makes one distinguishable from any other person. A trademark represents the name and reputation of the manufacturer. For instance, a particular model of a car produced by a certain auto company exhibits specific characteristics in accordance with its company's name and reputation. So Christ's making of true disciples reflects the good name and excellent reputation of the Master Worker.

His name and reputation were His disciples' mark of distinction as they lived out His life in this world. "Christ's *name* is their *watchword*, their *badge* of distinction, their *bond* of union, the *authority* of their course of action, and the *source* of their success. Nothing that does not bear His *superscription* is to be recognized in His kingdom" *(The Desire of Ages,* p. 826; italics supplied).

PEOPLE, THEN PROGRAMS

His disciples' devotion and loyalty resulted from His primary focus on people rather than on programs. He made His indelible mark on persons, who then reproduced His life and ministry. He well knew that the success of a program—no matter how great it might be—depends essentially on the quality of the workers responsible for its implementation. Whenever I hear a debate on the effectiveness or ineffectiveness of a program, I often feel compelled to shift the focus from programs to people. For it is, to a large degree, committed and competent individuals who make or break a program. Leaders who fail to learn this essential lesson end up paying dearly for their mistake.

It is true that a plan may have a great potential for success. But what is usually our reaction if it fails? Often we find ourselves faulting the plan rather than the individuals in charge. It does happen that an inferior plan can flourish in the hands of a quality worker, and a superior one may fail in the hands of an inferior worker. On the one hand, we all know that a good teacher can take a dull and despised subject and make it enticing to the students. On the other hand, a dull teacher may take an interesting subject and make it quite boring. In grade school I excelled in math, a subject I had not liked that much before, but a good teacher made it so understandable and interesting that I could not but enjoy it.

MARKED FOR LIFE

Jesus was the best Teacher and Disciple Maker who ever lived, and He certainly left His mark on His disciples. He was what He taught them to be, and He lived and imparted such to them. His mission was a marked mission, uniquely distinguished from any other, and His disciples were marked persons, carrying the marks of His life and ministry in their lives. Paul presented to the Galatians the marks of Christ in his body as undisputed proof of his absolute devotion and loyalty to Christ. "From now on let no one trouble me," he writes, "for I bear in my body the marks of the Lord Jesus" (Gal. 6:17).

Stigmata is the Greek word Paul used for "marks." There was then the practice of sometimes branding slaves, captives, and soldiers with the identifying mark of the master or commanding officer. Besides the physical scars of hardship and persecution for the sake of His Master, the apostle presented the marks of Christ's character stamped upon his life. In every way he was marked for life in complete submission and service to the Saviour. This was in accordance with the marked life of the Master. He was marked on the cross with scars that will ever remain in His body—sacred scars that speak eloquently of His complete commitment to us. We have the holy honor of sharing these marks of love and sacrifice with Christ when we, as His true disciples, live and suffer for His cause.

THE MARK OF CHRISTLIKENESS

Christ stamps the marks of His character and likeness in every aspect of our lives. The marks of a "Christlike life [are] the *most powerful* argument that can be advanced in favor of Christianity" (Ellen G. White, *Testimonies for the Church,* vol. 9, p. 21; italics supplied).

Such marks cannot be hidden, but are seen and felt by all those with whom we come in contact. There are telling signs, then, that His life has indeed transformed our lives and that we have become a genuine reflection of Him. Christ reveals Himself through us to the extent that those who meet us meet Him. We are marked by His sweet aroma, diffusing the "fragrance of His knowledge in every place" (2 Cor. 2:14), and we are stamped as His epistle, "known and read by all men . . . written not with ink but by the Spirit of the living God, not on tablets of stone but on tablets of flesh, that is, of the heart" (2 Cor. 3:2, 3).

The Holy Spirit fashions this invisible insignia into our inner being and makes it visible through a Christlike life. That is how others will know that Christ and His claims are for real, because they have become real in those whom they can observe. "The badge of Christianity is not an outward sign, not the wearing of a cross or a crown, but it is that which reveals the union of man with God," writes Ellen White. "By the power of His grace manifested in the transformation of character the world is to be convinced that God has sent His Son as its Redeemer" *(The Ministry of Healing,* p. 470).

Such marks were so recognizable in the discipled lives of Peter and John that even their enemies "realized that they had been with Jesus" (Acts 4:13). The Master's life was now so indelibly marked in their lives that the way they spoke and behaved betrayed His marked influence on them. Even the very atmosphere His Spirit exerted around them revealed His likeness and His undeniable divine presence.

"The most important work of Christ prior to His death and resurrection was the selection and training of the men who would represent Him in the world," writes Everett Harrison. "These disciples were the *product of the Lord.* They *bore His stamp" (A Short Life of Christ,* p. 136; italics supplied). The people around them in Antioch recognized those early disciples of Christ to be His unmistakable product, for in their lives and witness they bore His indelible stamp.

"SEE HOW THESE CHRISTIANS LOVE ONE ANOTHER"

That is why Christ's faithful followers were first called "Christians" (Acts 11:26) in that ancient city of Antioch. The heathen could not but nickname them such, because Christ was all they talked about, lived for, and emulated. They overflowed with Christ. The nickname Christian was at first used to deride them, but with time it stuck to them, becoming their badge of honor. It implied that they were extensions of Christ, so to speak, living His life in their lives.

The most distinguishing and all-embracing marks of Christ's mission of growing disciples is love that is evidenced in a Christlike character. The genuine manifestation of His love will be found in the lives of His disciples and will be noticed inside and outside the church. If we are to love the world for Christ, we must first love each other in Christ and love each other *as* He has loved us. That is His new commandment to us: "As I have loved you, that you also love one another" (John 13:34). This goes beyond merely loving others as ourselves to loving them as Christ loves us. Loving each other this way is potent and pervasive, and Jesus assures us that "by this all will know that you are My disciples" (verse 35).

This is the clearest evidence to all that we have taken upon ourselves the characteristics of our Master: He has marked His love in our lives, making us people who not merely profess it but indeed possess it. The early Christians loved each other with this *agapē* love as Jesus loved them, and the Gentiles around them were utterly amazed, simply because they had never before seen such love in action.

This was a contrasting and unusual phenomenon in their world. No wonder Tertullian, one of the early Church Fathers, commented: "The heathen are wont to exclaim with wonder, 'See how these Christians love one another,' for they hate one another; 'and how they are ready to die for one another,' for they are ready to kill one another" (quoted in Michael J. Wilkins, *Following the Master,* p. 233). This is the rare spectacle and distinguishing mark that is possessed only by those who are possessed by Christ. It not only distinguishes us but also draws others to the Christ who lives in our lives.

COMMUNION AND COMMUNITY

I remember visiting a church some years ago whose members genuinely demonstrated love that was distinguishable and drawing. My family and I were astounded. Although it was our first visit and we hardly knew anyone there, these total strangers received us with open arms and hearts. They made us feel so at home, so loved, so included and accepted, that we felt as though they had been our friends for years. And that loving atmosphere extended beyond the church service to the afternoon fellowship and to caring contacts week after week.

Their continuous living demonstration of Christ's love—not just toward us, but toward each other—irresistibly drew us to that church. We wanted to be a part of their vibrant experience of living and sharing God's love. Their undeniably genuine love for visitors was simply the *overflow* of their genuine love for each other. This was not merely what the pastor pontificated, but what the laity practiced and what the people around them clearly felt.

It is obvious that making disciples for Christ would thrive in such a loving environment of communion and community. It was truly an atmosphere conducive of reciprocal caring, mutual trust, and a sense of belonging, where disciples may grow and mature, reaching their potential in the power of His Spirit. "This fellowship of kindred spirits became the primary means by which the disciples were trained," Robert Coleman explains. "Just as Jesus had lived closely with His followers, so now the gath-

ered community of believers formed an ongoing communion with His Spirit" *(The Master Plan of Evangelism,* p. 59).

There is a tremendous need for this experience in
many churches as well as in society as a whole. There is
such deep hunger for this that when people are finally
gripped by its tangible reality, they are pulled into it as air
is sucked into a vacuum. Zechariah 8:23 presents this ideal
that God envisions for His faithful people: "In those days
ten men from every language of the nations shall grasp the
sleeve of a Jewish man, saying 'Let us go with you, for we
have heard that God is with you.'"

Yes, it is the loving and transforming presence of God in
our lives that has the drawing power. People hold on to us,
desperately wanting to have what we have in Christ. And
this cannot be humanly concocted. It is divinely created by
the power of the indwelling Christ. God's people's "greatest
drawing power would be not in themselves as such, but in
the fact that God was with them. That is the most powerful
and the only way to draw others to God" (Philip G. Samaan,
Portraits of the Messiah in Zechariah, pp. 99, 100).

"THE STRONGEST ARGUMENT IN FAVOR OF THE GOSPEL"

Imagine what would happen to our churches if we
truly love each other *as* Jesus Himself loves us. His uncon-
ditional and self-sacrificing love can be manifested only
through the lives of His true disciples. Love reaches out to
people for their own sake as people, not because of condi-
tions met or favors received but because such love is the
principle of action. Such love can saturate the human heart
and course through it to others because it is replenished

and inundated by the great reservoir of God's love.

A lot of promotional material is printed and publicity releases distributed in order to attract others to attend churches. And that has its place. However, the most powerful promotion and publicity is the existence of an authentically loving Christian community. This kind of promotion does not end up in disappointment, because they witness that the profession and possession of God's love have indeed become one and the same. Indeed, "the *strongest argument* in favor of the gospel is a *loving and lovable* Christian" *(The Ministry of Healing,* p. 470; italics supplied). And that is the only kind of love which can forge a Christian community of true disciples to impact the world.

OUR LOVE ANCHORED IN HIS LOVE

The best of human love is simply incapable of doing that, no matter how well intentioned it may be. Here is what David Watson says about it: "Human love, for all its powerful outflow of emotions, is basically self-centered and self-seeking. It desires to have, to possess, to capture; it does not serve and give. Human love is reluctant to release the object of that love for the good of the whole. Human love manipulates people and situations to achieve its end. It is restless, insatiable, and destructive of true fellowship" *(Called and Committed,* p. 34).

This is the dilemma of human love that is not anchored in God's love. And no matter how much we may attempt to experience a truly loving community, without being secure in His love we would be discouraged and hurt. There is always a risk involved in loving relationships. Watson again: "Paradoxically, the more deeply we commit ourselves to loving fellowship with others, the more we shall be hurt." Why? Because "as sinners we shall fail one another again and again" *(ibid., p. 33)*.

However, as we open our lives to Christ's love we shall "accept, with love and understanding, the foibles and frailties of others. . . . Jesus had to bear all this from His disciples; if we want to follow Him we must do the same" *(ibid.)*. Unless we actualize the first part of what Christ said, "As I have loved you," we cannot really experience the second part, "Love one another" (John 13:34). "Christ is the great center, and they would approach one another just in proportion as they approached the center" *(The Desire of Ages, p. 296)*. And from Him extended cords of love to each one of the diverse 12 disciples, pulling them to Him and to each other.

Growth takes time, and Christ's patient and persistent pull on them with His cords of love eventually pulled them together in one accord. Without His pull of love, whatever love we may imagine we have deteriorates into selfishness. Without His love we will experience all sorts of self-centered reactions, such as becoming disappointed, taking offence, thwarted expectations, getting hurt. And consequently, we either hold tighter to our masks of pretension or crawl back into our safe shells of isolation, vowing not to be hurt again.

CHARACTERISTICS OF A TRUE DISCIPLE

As we have been discussing, the most distinguishing mark of fruitful disciples is, namely, Christlikeness as it is expressed in *agapē* love. This love is the glue that holds everything together. From this mark springs forth other important characteristics.

THE MARK OF THE MISSION

1. A true disciple is someone called by Christ Himself.
Of course, He may use human agencies and circumstances to give such a call. Nevertheless, it is still His choice and call. "You did not choose Me," He declared to His disciples, "but I chose you" (John 15:16). And it is true that He desires that all will become His disciples, but He calls only those who respond to Him and receive His message. Such are the qualifications for answering Christ's call.

2. A true disciple is someone called to Christ Himself.
It is a very personal call, not to a philosophy or a program, but exclusively to His person. He calls us to a life of heart-to-heart and mind-to-mind communion with Him, to a life of love and loyalty to Him. Dietrich Bonhoeffer aptly put it: "When we are called to follow Christ, we are summoned to an *exclusive attachment to his person . . . .* Discipleship means *adherence to Christ*" (*The Cost of Discipleship,* p. 63; italics supplied).

Contrary to today's many cult leaders who use fear and force to intimidate their followers into forced compliance, Jesus makes it very easy for His disciples to leave if they so choose. Those of His disciples who "went back and walked with Him no more" (John 6:66) were not pursued by Jesus and shamed into coming back. He wanted those to stay with Him who really wanted to stay. It was a personal and intimate thing to be called to Christ, and such a wonderful thing could not and should never be contrived or coerced.

And such is the unique personal call of Jesus. The Greek philosophers as well as the rabbis of His day called their disciples to a teaching, a philosophy, or a cause, but *He called them to Himself.* He who said "Come to Me" and

"Follow Me" is Himself "the way, the truth, and the life" (John 14:6). Everything in their lives was to center in and around His life. Confucius, Buddha, Socrates, Muhammad, and Marx called their followers to be loyal to their *ideas*, but Jesus called His disciples to love Him and be loyal to *Him*.

3. A true disciple is someone who is loyal to our loving Lord and obedient to His will. Such staunch loyalty to Him is called forth from His selfless love to us. This implies that we love to remain in Him, submit to Him, and obey Him in all things. We choose to abide in Him daily so that He may continuously sustain us and make us fruitful. An undeniable link exists between devotion and love to Christ and loyalty and obedience to Him. He who said "If you love Me" also said "Keep My commandments" (John 14:15). And He who said "If you keep My commandments" said also "You will abide in My love" (John 15:10).

Obedience to Christ confirms our love for Him. And the reason it seems so hard to advance in our love for Christ is because we are reluctant to obey Him. It is precisely that deficiency in obedience which disables discipleship. You see, formation and responsible obedience are indispensable ingredients of discipleship. Bill Hull concurs when he asserts that in ignoring obedience to the Lord's mandate to make disciples, we make discipleship ineffective. "The words 'to obey' have been referred to as *the great omission in the Great Commission*. The great omission is that we have not really made disciples if we have not taught them to obey. . . . Indeed, God wants our love. But love is primarily a verb, an action which is demonstrated through obedience" *(Jesus Christ Disciple Maker,* pp. 11, 12; italics supplied).

4. A true disciple is someone who is productive. Like fruit that is produced by the very force of the inner life of the branch, so Christ's life flows into our lives and makes them fruitful. A barren disciple is a contradiction in terms, for to be a disciple is to share in the fruitful life of the Master. "It is just as unthinkable for a disciple to be fruitless as it is for a healthy apple tree not to yield its natural harvest," Hull asserts. "You can indeed recognize a disciple by the results he produces in his own life *and* in the lives of others" *(ibid., p. 12)*.

That, Jesus said, is why I "appointed you that you should go and bear fruit, and that your fruit should remain" (John 15:16). To be fruitful disciples is to multiply in the lives of others the fruit that Christ has reproduced in us. And this fruit is of such quality that it will endure to reproduce more and more. Fruit bearers reproduce their own kind—fruit bearers. And if we are fruit bearers, those whom we reproduce cannot be fruit consumers, but fruit bearers also, living branches participating in the life and abundance of Christ.

5. A true disciple is someone who is called to serve, to sacrifice, and to suffer for Christ. We are to follow our Master's example in serving others, just as He "did not come to be served, but to serve, and to give His life a ransom for many" (Matt. 20:28). Prior to that Jesus said, "Whoever desires to become great among you, let him be your servant" (verse 26). There is no place in discipleship for selfish ambition and self-aggrandizement. Such manifestations are sure disqualifiers.

Our Lord did not come to this world to lord it over others, for He emptied Himself and, in humility, became obedient even unto death (see Phil. 2:7, 8). Such condescension was indeed costly to Christ, and in following Him we must count the cost, for it will cost us dearly as well. Consider the suffering He endured and the ultimate sacrifice He offered. It is our badge of honor to live, suffer, and sacrifice for Him. "When Christ calls a man," Dietrich Bonhoeffer wrote, "He calls him to come and die" *(The Cost of Discipleship,* p. 99). The beautiful crown in glory emerges from the bloodstained cross at Golgotha.

6. *A true disciple is someone who possesses inner peace and joy,* confirming others in and convicting them of the reality of life in Christ. After everything is said and done, a life of genuine peace and inner joy is certainly the acid test that declares to the world that we are possessed by Christ's peace and joy. Content and secure in Christ, we possess His peace that "surpasses all understanding" (Phil. 4:7). "Peace I leave with you, My peace I give to you;" Jesus said to His disciples, "not as the world gives do I give to you. Let not your heart be troubled, neither let it be afraid" (John 14:27).

The lives of true disciples are not marked by anxious disposition and troubled countenance. True peace in the life is seen most clearly and authentically in spite of troubled and trying times. A scene of a dove and her young nestled precariously on a branch extending above a raging river gives us a vivid portrait of true peace.

Jesus also spoke to His disciples of joy. Their lives were to be marked by inner joy. "These things [abiding in His love and fellowship] I have spoken to you, that My joy may remain in you, and that your joy may be full" (John 15:11). Joy and happiness are not synonymous. Happiness is what the United States Constitution encourages us to pursue. But no matter how much we think we have attained it, happiness seems fluctuating, fleeting, and superficial, at the mercy of circumstances.

However, joy is something inward and abiding. "It is the inward, profound, and serene sort of joy that springs forth from His joy abiding in us" (Philip G. Samaan, *Christ's Way to Spiritual Growth,* p. 45). Such joy clearly marked the lives of Paul and Silas. Although they were severely beaten and thrown into prison in Philippi, at midnight the walls of that dark dungeon reverberated with the joyous sound of their singing (see Acts 16:22-25).

7. *A true disciple is someone who possesses spiritual power and exercises spiritual authority*. There is a dearth of this in Christ's body today. Of course, there are always those who have a knack for leadership, those who rise to power in any situation. There were many of those in Christ's time too, yet He called them not, choosing to call those He could mold into His image. Our Lord, more than anything else, is interested in life—His life reproduced in our lives. He seeks lives that are empty of self, submissive to His authority, and filled with His power.

There are always church leaders who get promoted to the top by sheer talent and flair for leadership. Unfortunately, some of them give the impression that they are indispensable and that God is indeed fortunate to have them in His entourage. I once heard a leader allude to how fortunate the church was to benefit by his leadership skills. He insinuated that if He had not been leading the church, he would have become a chief executive officer of a giant corporation.

We must never forget that the power God recognizes

in any disciple is never human power, but is ever the power of His Spirit in the life. And spiritual authority flows from a transformed spiritual life. People around us must recognize His powerful presence and His divine atmosphere around us so that when we speak and act, we speak and act in His authority, and when we pray and intercede, we do so prevailingly, as He did. This is not derived from acquiring great knowledge or anything else, but solely from a life of prevailing with God. That is what is needed today in our lives to transform our churches and our world. "Not by might nor by power, but by My Spirit, says the Lord of hosts" (Zech. 4:6).

8. A true disciple of Christ is someone who lives for the supreme purpose of glorifying God. All the preceding marks and characteristics of a true disciple are there to glorify God. They are what make a disciple's life glow with the light of God's glory. Jesus said, "Let your light so shine before men, that they may see your good works and glorify your Father in heaven" (Matt. 5:16).

Our transformed lives, authenticated by and manifested through our good works of obedience, bring glory to God. And the good work that brings great glory to Christ is to obey His command to reproduce and multiply disciples after His likeness. Thus the more such fruit-bearing disciples are reproduced, so as to be reproduced in others, the more God is glorified. "By this My Father is glorified," Jesus said, "that you bear much fruit" (John 15:8).

9. A true disciple is neither born nor made, but is first born of the Spirit, then trained and equipped to do the work of Christ. "The belief that disciples are born, not made," writes Hull, "leads one to conclude that disciple making is evangelism" *(The Disciple Making Pastor,* p. 59). Making converts and adding members to the church is good, but it is only the first step and must always lead to disciple-making.

The commission given by Christ to make disciples must become our top priority among many competing demands, for everything is connected to it and dependent on it. And it was given for a good reason, because evangelism will falter unless converts are discipled and, in their turn, disciple others. Indeed, the production and multiplication of fruit-bearing disciples is what is desperately needed today in the body of Christ. It is the distinguishing mark that must be indelibly stamped in every believer and must transcend the activities of every church. Nothing more and nothing less is worthy to carry forth the message of the Master's mission.

CHAPTER FOUR

The MESSAGE of the Mission

In our great democracy presidential hopefuls seem to be in a mode of perpetual campaigning. As we endure one presidential campaign after another, politicians scramble to come up with a winning message that is worded just right to attract the electorate's elusive support. Pro-life, pro-choice, no more taxes, gun control, welfare reform, health care, the economy—to name just a few. They search desperately for a pertinent message to capture people's imagination. Some seem to shift from one message to another, hoping to nail down one that may fit the popular mood at the moment. To others a catchy message proves elusive, except they just seem to be obsessed with the idea of becoming president.

THE SAME MESSAGE OF HOPE

Amid all such ambitions to reach the pinnacle of earthly power, we should consider Jesus, the King of the universe, who did not grasp on to His rightful position of divine power, but in love emptied Himself to save a doomed world. He was heaven's Messenger *and* Message of hope to a hopeless humanity. His message of the gospel never varied from the foundation of the world. It is the good news that He came to seek and save those who are lost. Satan is a thief who came "to steal, and to kill, and to destroy," but Jesus came that "they may have life, and that they may have it more abundantly" (John 10:10).

It is the best news, indeed, that Jesus came to this dying world so that in Him we may have abundant and eternal life. This is the good news that He wanted His disciples to disperse throughout the world. It is the message that is to be propagated through the method of spiritual reproduction, causing it to spread like fire in dry stubble, engulfing the world.

THE WAY, THE TRUTH, AND THE LIFE

Jesus, in coming to this world, was not only the Messenger but also the Message, because of this He was utterly unique among the world's religious leaders. Some pointed to *a way*, but He is *the Way*. Others claimed to discover *a truth*, but He is *the Truth* embodied. Yet others dreamed of *renewing life,* but He is *the Life abundant and eternal*. Whereas others *dreamed of bringing salvation* to specific peoples, He ever remains *the Saviour of the whole world*.

"Behold! The Lamb of God who takes away the sin of the world!" (John 1:29). This was what John the Baptist was compelled by the Spirit to exclaim as for the first time he saw Jesus approach him. Jesus Christ, God's divine Son and messenger, came to Planet Earth to bring in His person the eternal message of redemption, not merely to a nation, but to the entire world. His life, death, resurrection, and heavenly intercession testify eloquently to the glorious truth. This was precisely what the message of His mission was: His life fully given to the world.

A day later John the Baptist again directed the attention of his disciples to Jesus as God's universal Message to the world (verses 35, 36). Apparently there was something special about His personality that drew Andrew and John to Jesus, for it is recorded that they immediately followed Him (verse 37). It is clear that they were not merely curious about a particular point of doctrine, but in Him as a person. They had more than enough of dry doctrinal debate from the religious leaders. Now, in a refreshing way, they were witnessing the living demonstration of God's message to humanity in the person of Christ. And this good news was contagious, for Andrew could not wait to tell his brother, Simon, about his joy of finding the Messiah.

THE MASTER IS THE MESSAGE

No wonder, then, when He asked them *what* they sought, they instead unhesitatingly responded as to *whom* they sought. They were so interested in Jesus that they wanted to stay with Him where He lived. And Jesus responded, "Come and see" (verses 38-39). Not even a slight hint of coercion or manipulation was evident in His invitation. "Come and observe for yourselves, and then freely decide if you desire to become more involved and committed to My cause." So they went and remained with Him, witnessing a living demonstration of who He was and how He lived. In Himself Jesus was to demonstrate the Message before them so that they too would do likewise in their own lives.

Indeed, His message was to be manifested to the world, not through a mere myriad of methods, but through the lives of men and women transformed by the life of *the* Man. E. M. Bounds said: "The church is looking for *better methods*: God is looking for *better men" (Power Through Prayer,* p. 11; italics supplied). Christ intended that the *what* of His mission was to be seen and demonstrated by the *who* of the mission. The gospel "was embodied in Emmanuel's own life and work," Robert Coleman explains. "The message found expression in the way He lived and ministered, and confirmed in His decisive defeat of death" *(The Master Plan of Discipleship,* p. 25).

THE ETERNAL BEST AND MOST

This message was not to be contained in one place or limited to one people, but it was to be on the march until its claims were communicated to everyone everywhere. In no other place in the Scriptures are the substance and the scope of Christ's message better expressed than in John 3:16: "For God so loved the world that He gave His only begotten Son, that whoever believes in Him should not perish but have everlasting life."

The *quality* of God's message of love in Christ is the *absolute best* that Heaven could give to this world. Its *quantity* is the *absolute most* that Heaven could pour out in one Gift upon humanity. And its *duration* is *eternity itself.* This eternal link with Christ will never be broken. It is indeed the Son who embodies in Himself the totality of God's message of salvation to all humanity. The *what* of this mission was seen in the context of and demonstrated by the *who* of this mission.

THE SIMPLE INVITATION

Its living demonstration was vastly different from the stale theories and conflicting arguments of the rabbis.

There was power in the simple invitation to "come and see" for themselves Christ's life and ministry. There was no need to enter any controversy, use manipulation, or apply any pressure to coerce Christ's first two disciples, Andrew and John, to know more about the Messiah. They were "moved by an irresistible impulse" to follow Him (*The Desire of Ages,* p. 138). The sheer force of His godly personality and pure character drew them to Himself. Yet they were completely free to go and observe for themselves, decide to stay, or turn back.

What a valuable lesson to learn in the way we introduce people to Christ and the church! The tendency is to hurry them to sign up on the "dotted line" and to commit them to more than they are prepared to commit themselves at a given time in their spiritual journey. If Christ's Spirit overflows from our lives and churches, we would be less anxious and more secure in inviting others simply to come and have a look. Such a simple and sincere invitation assures us that Christ's life, demonstrated in His body, would give them the greatest drawing power to stay and come again for more.

It has been proven again and again that whatever proceeds from love works out best in the long run, but whatever is coerced is eventually counterproductive. Jesus made it easy to say no, for His love was never controlling or pushy. He did not present His message as an offer that no one could resist. When people are pressured into commitment to Christ, "the recruit normally takes off like a rocket, only to fall back later to the earth like a rock. After such a misfire, restoration is nearly impossible, a very messy business" (*Jesus Christ Disciple Maker,* p. 19).

Philip, who went and saw Jesus for himself, apparently learned this valuable lesson. He shared with his friend Nathanael his initial experience with Jesus, inviting him *as* he was invited simply to "come and see." To come and have a look and then decide freely for himself. That was just the appropriate reaction to alleviate his friend's doubt and prejudice. No arduous arguments, no elaborate explanations. The subject of attraction is so superior that there is no need for a clever promotional job. "The proof is in the pudding," as the saying goes. Just come, see, and decide for yourself as to what the Spirit impresses you to do. It is wisest to introduce others to Christ this way. "Philip entered into no controversy [with Nathanael]. . . . He did not ask him to accept another's testimony, but to behold Christ for himself" *(The Desire of Ages,* pp. 140, 141).

This also reveals clearly how the foundation of the first Christian church was solidly established: personal initiative. Those first disciples never contemplated the thought of relegating the joy of sharing Christ to the spiritual leaders of their day. "These examples should teach us the importance of personal effort, of making direct appeals to our kindred, friends, and neighbors. There are those who for a lifetime have professed to be acquainted with Christ, yet who have never made a personal effort to bring even one soul to the Saviour. They leave all the work for the minister" *(ibid.,* p. 141).

A church member and I were studying the Bible for a few months with a married young couple, and even though they were enjoying the studies, they were quite apprehensive about attending the church. Curious, we finally asked them about their lingering reluctance to worship with us. They confided that their only concern was that if they set foot in the church, they would feel pressured to go back, and they simply were not ready for that.

We hastened to reassure them that they would not be coerced in any way, that they could simply come and see for themselves what the church experience was like. "Try us out and see how it goes," we said reassuringly. "Of course, you will always be welcome; however, if you choose not to come back, we would understand and continue to be friends." When they heard this, they felt quite relieved and at ease to come and see, and liking what they saw, they continued coming. A year later they were baptized.

This is the simple way of how Jesus launched His great mission to spiritually reproduce Himself and His mission in the first disciples: the invitation to spend time with Him, observing what He was about and what He planned to do. As the Messiah, He knew that this was the most important mission ever embarked on in the entire history of humanity, yet He was never in the least anxious to push Himself or ideas on others. "Jesus preferred planting a few seeds of thought and then nurturing them through experience" (*Jesus Christ Disciple Maker*, p. 33). In such initial thoughts Jesus introduced His first disciples to His plans for the task at hand.

THE BIGGER PICTURE

After a few months of observing Him and learning from Him, the disciples were to look beyond themselves to the wider harvest. They were not to follow Jesus merely for their own spiritual benefit. Rather they would rise to the challenge of spreading His message for the benefit of the world. That was His ultimate task at hand. However, Jesus did not overwhelm them with it, but progressively unfolded it to them, corresponding to the level of their learning experience. That is why the Great Commission (Matt. 28:19, 20) was preceded by several preliminary ones.

Again and again Jesus kept reinforcing the great vision before them, engaging them in hands-on outreach activities, thus increasing their understanding of what they were called to do. For example, He challenged them repeatedly to fish for souls (Mark 1:16, 17) and to labor in the harvest (Matt. 9:36-38). Everything that Jesus did in the process of training His disciples was to prepare them to carry out the Great Commission to "go therefore and make disciples of all the nations" (Matt. 28:19).

The message of salvation was not to be narrowly confined or jealously guarded, but to be fully shared. "Behold, I say to you, lift up your eyes and look at the fields, for they are already white for harvest!" (John 4:35). This was the challenge that Jesus gave His 12 disciples—to lift their eyes beyond, to see the great potential, to perceive things from His perspective. Sometimes we are tempted to blame the hardness of the fields of labor or the challenge of the message, but Christ pointed out that the problem was with the laborers. The fields were ripe for the harvest, Heaven's message was the most wonderful good news to bear, but trained laborers were desperately needed to carry such a message to a dying world.

Trained and mobilized laborers is what is greatly needed. Such laborers who will go beyond simple outreach, beyond baptizing and adding new converts to reproduction and multiplication of disciples. That was the divine genius of carrying the message of Christ to the whole world through disciples who would teach new converts to observe all things that their Master had commanded them (Matt. 28:20). "Christ not only outlined their work, but *gave them their message.* . . . The disciples were to teach what Christ had taught" *(The Desire of Ages,* p. 826; italics supplied).

To make disciples implies the dynamic of not only reproducing disciples, but multiplying them as well. "The church was commanded to produce a kind of person who would obey Christ, evangelize his world, and set off a chain reaction called multiplication" *(The Disciple Making Pastor,* p. 194). Reproduction must always lead to multiplication. If the convert whom the Spirit helped us reproduce is not equipped to likewise reproduce other disciples, then the process of multiplication is thwarted. Of course, both reproduction and multiplication are musts in order not to short-circuit the divine chain reaction of the ultimate goal of reaching doomed humanity with the message of salvation.

ESSENTIAL STEPS IN TRAINING

The following experience will help summarize what has been presented so far and serve to introduce the coming chapters as we continue to consider the different steps of Christ's way of making fruit-bearing disciples.

Living through some long and frigid winters in the flat terrain of southwestern Michigan, my family decided that cross-country skiing seemed the thing to do if we wanted to get outside and enjoy the abundant snow. *If we cannot beat the snow, then let us enjoy it,* we thought. Our young daughter, never having skied before, had to learn methodically and patiently how to do it. Certain steps come to mind that seemed to logically fall in place in the training process.

The *first step* was to explain to her *what* this activity was about. My "message" to her was to "come and see" what it was like, to discover the potential it had to help us enjoy the cold winters. This step corresponds to the basic idea in this chapter of sharing the *message* in the process of making disciples.

The *second step* was to explain to her *why* she needed to try out cross-country skiing, what the motivation and rationale for it were. Of course, the rationale was to get out, make the dreary winters more enjoyable, and stay fit and healthy in the process. This step corresponds with the next chapter, which deals with the *motivation* for growing disciples.

In the *third step* I started demonstrating to our daughter *how* to ski. I showed her how to use the poles, how to put the skis on, how to move, and so on. She observed me showing her different aspects, asked questions, and tried to get a feel for the equipment. This step corresponds with the chapter on the *method* of growing disciples.

In the *fourth step* we ventured to ski together. She fell a few times as expected, but she tried diligently to imitate me as she followed behind. It was not something to behold, to be sure, but it was at least a promising beginning. Under my watchful eyes she was trying . . . and slowly getting better at skiing. This step corresponds with the chapter on the *modeling* of growing disciples.

In the *fifth step* I let her ski all by herself. I would ski a distance ahead of her and would then encourage her to ski toward me. She would move ahead, trying to stay up as she negotiated a corner or picked up speed coming down a bank. When she would finally get to where I was—full of trepidation and excitement—we would go over what happened and try again. This step corresponds with the chapter about Christ's sending the Twelve on their own as His *messengers*. They were to report to Him and be evaluated, but He let go of them and let them do it on their own. With time and practice, our daughter was able to ski by herself.

In the *sixth step* she "mastered" skiing. Of course, even though I was not physically present with her, she was certain I was with her in spirit and very much interested in her progress. This step corresponds with the chapter in which we will discuss how under the guidance of their Master, the disciples became *masters* of Christ's mission.

Finally, the last chapter deals with the *movement* of the mission. When the disciples were ready to be deployed, Jesus assured them that although He would be leaving them bodily, they would remain in Him through His Spirit. The promised Holy Spirit would empower them to *move* His mission of reproducing and multiplying fruit-bearing disciples to the farthest corners of the earth.

CHAPTER FIVE

The MOTIVATION
of the Mission

On the snowy afternoon of January 13, 1982, shortly after takeoff from Washington National Airport (now Ronald Reagan Washington National Airport), Air Florida Flight 90 suddenly plunged into the frozen waters of the Potomac River. Miraculously, some passengers managed to escape from the plane, only to find themselves bobbing in the frigid water covered with ice chunks. Rescuers in a helicopter hovering over this chaotic scene tried desperately to save the crash victims, who seemed too weak to reach or to hold on to the lowered lifeline.

But there was a man in the freezing river who chose repeatedly to bypass his turn to grab the lifeline in order that he could help rescue his fellow passengers. Every single time it reached him, he gave it to someone else. When it was lowered to him yet another time, he was nowhere to be seen. He had been overcome by paralyzing cold and sheer exhaustion.

THE REASON FOR THE RESCUE

I recalled that unforgettable experience recently as I strolled by that Potomac River location on a cold winter day. Gripped again by such a selfless and heroic act, I thought of Christ's supreme sacrifice on the cross to rescue me and doomed humanity. The *motivation* of the man in the water was altruistic human caring for strangers who were in desperate need. The *motivation* of the Man on the cross was pure divine love—even for His enemies. "But God demonstrates His own love toward us, in that while we were still sinners, Christ died for us" (Rom. 5:8). Such divine love filling our hearts is and must be the motivating factor in reaching others for Christ, regardless of their condition. Our deep gratitude to God and their desperate need for salvation provide us with the overwhelming rationale and the greatest incentive for selfless action.

Filled with gratitude to Christ and overwhelmed by all that He has done for us, we feel driven to do something for Him in response. Christ affirms that in ministering to Him we minister to others, for He says that "inasmuch as you did it to one of the least of these My brethren, you did it to Me" (Matt. 25:40). Therefore, we are moved by our love for Christ to love others, because we see Him in the least of them. And in ministering to them we are indeed ministering to Christ Himself. No matter how much we profess that we love Him, in reality, we love Him only as much as we love the least person around us. For a moment focus on a particular person in your life whom you love the least. This is how much you love Jesus. Think about it.

I once heard a preacher promising his listeners all the riches of heaven as an incentive to give up their material possessions—as an offering. What is our real incentive for becoming fruitful disciples of Christ? Peter asked a similar question of Jesus: "See, we have left all and followed You.

Therefore what shall we have?" (Matt. 19:27). Paul answers such a question this way: "But what things were gain to me, these I have counted loss for Christ. But indeed I also count all things loss for the excellence of the knowledge of Christ Jesus my Lord, for whom I have suffered the loss of all things, and count them as rubbish, that I may gain Christ" (Phil. 3:7, 8).

SHARING IN CHRIST'S MINISTRY OF RECONCILIATION

Our great reward is to know Jesus and to make Him known. All things fade into nothingness compared with knowing Him and spending eternity with Him. And there is nothing greater that can prepare us to be with Him in heaven than to work with Him in saving the lost on earth. No greater accomplishment exists than to become one with Jesus as He reproduces and multiplies His mission through us in advancing His kingdom. Nothing can give us more joy than to see the ones we lead to Jesus in the company of the redeemed, knowing that our witness played a part in their eternal salvation.

For all eternity we will contemplate the awesome reality of knowing that God used even us to be His partners in leading others from eternal death to eternal life—altering their destiny forever. And the profound impact of this will not fully sink in until that glorious day when we see such saved ones in Christ's presence.

And saving the lost is what Jesus came to this world to do. That was His loving motivation, and it must be ours as well. "For the Son of Man has come to seek and to save that which was lost" (Luke 19:10). "God did not send His Son into the world to condemn the world, but that the world through Him might be saved" (John 3:17). What a glorious privilege it is to be called to be partners with His Son in His ministry of reconciliation! Think about it: God has entrusted to us fallible human beings His own message of reconciliation to the world! "All this is from God, who through Christ reconciled us to himself and gave us the ministry of reconciliation; that is, in Christ God was reconciling the world to himself . . . and entrusting to us the message of reconciliation. So we are ambassadors for Christ, God making his appeal through us" (2 Cor. 5:18-20, RSV).

CHANNELS OVERFLOWING

LeRoy Eims says that Christ's disciples must be motivated in an inward and an outward direction. "Inwardly they must be motivated to have fellowship *with* Jesus Christ, and outwardly they must become witnesses *for* Jesus Christ" *(The Lost Art of Disciple Making,* p. 51). And these two aspects are and must always be inseparable: the outward ministry flows from the inward experience. Disciples feel so moved by their love and devotion to their Master that His love and life flow out spontaneously in reconciliation to others. "Our fruitfulness is the result of abiding in Christ," Eims asserts. Therefore, "fellowship with Christ must come first, for witnessing is not *overwork* but *overflow*. . . . Evangelism is what will keep your discipleship program alive. . . . The people of God are not *buckets* to be filled with all the riches of Christ, but they are *channels* of blessing to take Christ to the world" *(ibid.,* pp. 56, 57; italics supplied).

The potential of such human channels overflowing with Christ's loving ministry of reconciliation is limitless. And it is truly overflowing because of our overwhelming gratitude for what Christ has done for us. The Holy Spirit seizes us with the overwhelming compulsion to claim as many of the lost as possible.

PASSION TO SAVE THE LOST

Can you ever imagine firefighters being content to rescue no one or perhaps only one or two persons out of many trapped in a burning building? It is inconceivable that they would rest until they tried diligently to extricate the last person. We are God's "firefighters" on this doomed planet, and through us God wants to rescue as many of its inhabitants as He possibly can before it is too late. Soon a consuming fire will engulf this world with total devastation. How much more passionate, then, we ought to be to help rescue the perishing from eternal destruction. It is moving to see people passionately motivated to rescue endangered wildlife in all its forms. Yet it is amazing why Christians are not so motivated to help rescue the many endangered millions of precious souls whom Jesus created in His own image and redeemed with His own blood.

Many of us watched with disbelief the news of the hijacked Ethiopian Airlines Boeing 767 with 175 passengers on board. Running out of fuel, it was forced to crash in the Indian Ocean, near the shores of the island of Grand Comore, breaking into three pieces on impact. Vacationers watching this tragedy unfold before their eyes immediately took off—swimming, in canoes, boats, or using any means at their disposal—to rescue every individual they possibly could. And they were all total strangers to the crash victims.

Should we do any less to help rescue this hijacked planet with its billions of doomed passengers? No, for "the love of Christ leaves us no choice" (2 Cor. 5:14), as *The New English Bible* aptly puts it. J. B. Phillips renders it this way: "The very spring of our actions is the love of Christ." What a powerful way to describe this divine-human dynamic! The overwhelming love of Christ motivates us, seizes us, grabs us, compels us to act.

"HERE AM I! SEND ME"

As Jesus viewed the condition of people around Him, He said to His disciples, "The harvest truly is plentiful, but the laborers are few" (Matt. 9:37). We sometimes think that the main problem in accomplishing Christ's mission is the harvest. We say that people are sometimes very resistant to the gospel and unwilling to be rescued. Yet we do not think that the problem has to do with the labor force. However, Jesus tells us that there are only a *few* laborers and the desperate need is for many *more*. We often do not look at the harvest from His perspective. He sees through people's forbidding exteriors to their innermost struggles. He can read the sealed chapters in their lives like an open book, and He knows how desperately they need deliverance.

Little wonder, then, that Christ admonishes us to "pray the Lord of the harvest to send out laborers into His harvest" (Matt. 9:38). That is the prayer the Lord answers for sure. You and I can answer His earnest request by saying, "Yes, Lord, I want to respond by enlisting myself as a worker in the harvest." "Here am I! Send me" (Isa. 6:8). It is definitely His will to have us join His labor force. Knowing that God is "the Lord of the harvest" can greatly boost our motivation and confidence. He is the expert in charge of the work, yet He does it through us. He is totally engaged in this mission and commits all of heaven's resources to bring it to a glorious completion. The Lord, our leader, is the greatest source of our trust and motivation.

Jesus did not simply tell His disciples what He needed them to do. He also explained why He wanted them to do it. He is not like some arbitrary parents or leaders who demand of their children or followers what they want done without providing any answers or giving any explanations. "Do it because we said so, that's all," children sometimes hear, and when they try to understand why, they are rebuffed. They may obey out of ignorance and fear, but seldom out of inner conviction. This approach may even give immediate and superficial results, but not lasting and deep commitment. It often and ultimately leads to discouragement and disobedience, not to a compelling passion for a great cause.

Christ's rationale for calling us to be His fruit-bearing disciples is His desire to reach our doomed world with His gospel and prepare as many as possible to meet Him when He comes. That must be the driving force behind our loving obedience to His urgent command.

CHAPTER SIX

The METHOD of the Mission

In a culture of individualism we insist on doing things our way. We want things to go our way because we think therein lies our happiness and fulfillment in life. This reminds me of the popular song Frank Sinatra is known for, "My Way," and the other old song, "Oh, What a Beautiful Morning," in which the singer proclaims that everything is going his way. However, an experience of true happiness and fulfillment is found not in insisting on our way, but in submitting to Christ's way. He is the wise Guide to follow, for He is "the way, the truth, and the life" (John 14:6).

HE SENDS US AS HE WAS SENT

In this chapter we shall focus on *Christ's method* of making disciples. After having discussed the *what* and *why* of Christ's mission, we will now get into the *how* of it. And why *His* method? Obviously, because He is the Expert in this field, and in this specialty He knows exactly what He is doing. He is the Creator and the Redeemer, and He knows everything about advancing His message in the most efficient and effective way.

THE METHOD OF THE MISSION

After His resurrection Jesus said to His disciples, "As the Father has sent Me, I also send you" (John. 20:21). As far as our service to others is concerned, we are to emulate Christ's example. He came to this world seeking the lost with compassion and love. We are to reach out to lost people, teaching them about Jesus and training them to serve Him in His way. The saying is true that we serve best when we put the Saviour first. He bids us to come and follow Him as He trains us to serve as He served.

CHRIST'S PROGRAM IS PEOPLE

As Ellen White said: "Christ's method alone will give true success in reaching the people." *(The Ministry of Healing,* p. 143). In essence, Christ's method is *people*. We have to admit that no matter how sophisticated certain programs may be, without the right people involved, they do not amount to much. Even a most ingenious method or program cannot go very far if abused. All too often we hastily conclude that a perfectly good *program* was a failure. But in reality, the problem was not with the program as such, but with the *people* entrusted with the program. Indeed, it is much better to have an imperfect program with the right people than to have a perfect program with the wrong people. This is even much more important in following Christ's program of making disciples.

Che Guevara once said, "If our revolution is not aimed at changing people, then I am not interested." This is true more so when it comes to Christ's method of spiritual revolution. However, there is a big difference. Guevara's revolution aimed at changing people from the outside in; Christ aims at changing them from the inside out.

Absolutely nothing—or no one—can change the human heart but Christ.

Jesus was constantly pressured to launch human transformation from the outside—to overthrow the yoke of the Romans—but He would not yield. That is why Jesus invested so much of Himself in training the twelve. He knew that such personal investment would transform their hearts and make them more like Himself as He would transform the world through them. "When He [Jesus] set out to change the world, He chose only a dozen people to work with—not a cast of thousands. He packed value into every minute, every glance, every question, every encounter because He knew that out of little things come big ones" (Laurie Beth Jones, *Jesus, CEO,* p. 76).

By transforming them from within they became willing to put their lives on the line in their love and loyalty to Him. Forging such a strong bond with this small band, He would guarantee turning the world upside down. They were willing to sacrifice anything and everything for the cause of their Master. That was the genius of His strategy. With a handful of true believers He could encircle the globe with the everlasting gospel. As we noted earlier, Dietrich Bonhoeffer put it this way: "When Christ calls a man, He bids him come and die" *(The Cost of Discipleship,* p. 99).

Christ put all His eggs in one basket and went for broke, so to speak, counting on a handful of men. That was His program. That was His method. There was no other plan.

"The *most complete* illustration of Christ's *methods* as a teacher is found in His training of the twelve first disciples" (Ellen G. White, *Education,* p. 84; italics supplied). But it is not common to find such fruit-bearing disciples who reflect the Master's life and ministry. The biggest reason for such a problem is that "all too often we have relied on programs or materials or some other thing to do the job," LeRoy Eims explains. "The ministry is to be carried on by people, not programs. It is to be carried out by some*one* and not by some*thing*. Disciples cannot be mass produced. We cannot drop people into a 'program' and see disciples emerge at the end of the production line" *(The Lost Art of Disciple Making,* p. 45).

THE BIGGER PICTURE

But we are often too impatient with Christ's method of making disciples. We may regard it as a relic of the past to be admired in the museum of our memory, but not as a living reality in the real world. We would rather put church members through a crash course and expect quick results. Because we are so task-oriented and goal-obsessed, we crave quick results at any cost. We look more at the narrow and immediate, but less at the big and ultimate picture. It takes time, patience, and perseverance, to be sure, to follow Christ's example, but the dividends are all-encompassing and enduring.

I remember as a child watching my father and his friends build our stone house. During the first few weeks I remember my impatience at not seeing the walls, doors, and roof go up. For all I could see, these men digging the foundation were determined to reach bedrock. To me it seemed a waste of time and resources, but to them it was the most important part about the building. And indeed it is, for the solid foundation is what supports everything else. Jesus, the Master Builder, determined to invest all His resources in building the edifice of His mission, not on the shallow ground of passing popularity, but on the solid foundation of training His apostles. He was to count on their training. He entrusted them with His mission. He was to depend on their love, loyalty, experience, vision, and tenacity, under the power and guidance of the Holy Spirit, for the success of heaven's mission to Planet Earth.

Their mandate from their Commander was not merely to win Him converts as such, but to make disciples who would in turn produce disciples just as He had made them His disciples. A convert without discipleship does not remain a convert. Discipleship must not be an afterthought, for only in establishing people in Christ can they truly remain in Him. Paul knew this well. That is why he wrote: "As therefore you received Christ Jesus the Lord, so live in him, rooted and built up in Him and established in the faith, just as you were taught, abounding in thanksgiving" (Col. 2:6, 7, RSV).

ESSENTIAL STEPS IN MAKING DISCIPLES

Notice the steps the apostle Paul presents in the process of making disciples. It is serious business to become a living and fruit-bearing disciple. As we look at the following steps, we know without doubt that Paul makes a solid case for such priority.

1. *Receiving* **Christ.** His seed must be planted in our receptive hearts. No matter how wonderful the gospel of Christ is, it does not benefit us unless we receive it. It is tragic when we wax eloquent about how great Christ is without actually receiving Him in the heart.

2. *Living* **(walking) in Christ.** His seed grows more and more as the Holy Spirit supplies it with nourishment. This means we continue to live in Him as surely as we have received Him. Regardless of circumstances, we hold on to Jesus and grow in Him because we love and trust Him.

3. *Rooted* **in Christ.** His seed sends forth strong and deep roots as it germinates and flourishes in our hearts. In the Greek this implies firmness and continued stability. Thus we are to be rooted *firmly* in Christ, for our roots are not flimsy and shallow, but sturdy and deeply anchored in Him.

4. *Built up* **in Christ.** Anchored in Christ, our foundation, we continue to grow in our spiritual maturity. Established in Christ, we are assured of a solid structure that can withstand whatever may come.

5. *Established* **in the faith.** The Greek implies the idea of becoming spiritually mature and settled in Christ. This is a continuous and dynamic process of becoming confirmed, strengthened, and solidified in our relationship with Christ and His teachings.

6. *Abounding* **in thanksgiving.** When Christ becomes all in all to us, a spirit of gratitude overwhelms us, issuing forth in a continuous and overflowing stream of thankfulness. What a fitting way to wrap up what Paul said! Every step in the process of discipleship is motivated by a spirit of gratefulness to Christ. And when we are truly grateful, we are truly joyful. This is what gives glory to God. A powerful proof of spiritual maturity is when our actions are energized by such gratitude for and joy in the Lord.

THE FEW AND MANY:
SELECTIVITY AND CONCENTRATION

Robert Coleman describes Jesus' training of the few to reach the many as "the genius of His strategy." He writes: "Though He did what He could to help the multitudes, He had to devote Himself primarily to a few men, rather than the masses, in order that the masses could at last be saved" *(The Master Plan of Evangelism,* p. 33). Coleman refers to this as the "principle of selectivity and concentration." Applying this principle, he cautions, "will be slow, tedious, painful, and probably unnoticed by men at first, but the end result will be glorious, even if we don't live to see it." Then he gives the challenge that "one must decide where he wants his ministry to count—in the momentary applause of popular recognition or in the reproduction of his life in a few chosen men who will carry on his work after he has gone" *(ibid.,* pp. 35, 37).

The leaders who take this principle seriously in no way ignore the masses. On the contrary, they care enough to select the few for equipping and multiplying so that the masses may enjoy the most and best nurture and training available. For instance, consider a church congregation. What would be better for the members in the long haul? To have the pastor expend his limited energies on them? Or to multiply his efforts by concentrating his precious resources on equipping the few in order to minister to the many?

In answering these crucial questions, Bill Hull startles us by asserting that the pastor as a teacher/equipper is "called to work with the strong more than the weak." But he hastens to explain that "by training the well, he takes *better care* of and *strengthens* the weak." Because "the only

real hope for the weak is the disciple-making pastor's multiplying his influence through the preparation of Christians
for the work of service" *(The Disciple Making Pastor,* p. 74;
italics supplied).

The point is that the more fruit-bearing disciples the
church reproduces, the more nurture and training it exhibits
among its members. This way the productive pastor shares
with and multiplies in others his ministry so that they may
help him build up the body of Christ (Eph. 4:12). There is
absolutely no other rationale for the church to exist. Its very
reason for being is to make disciples. It is the very air it
breathes, and without this it simply suffocates. Making disciples is not to be thought of merely as the church's product, but its process and method—its way of life.

CHAPTER SEVEN

The MODELING of the Mission

I knew of a pastor who believed and practiced the principle of training the few to reach the many. His whole ministry was wrapped up in training his church members by example. Modeling what he taught was the heartbeat of his ministry. He lived by these words woven into all his instruction: "The church of Christ is organized for service. . . . Its members are soldiers, to be trained for conflict under the Captain of their salvation. . . . They [Christian leaders] are not only to minister to the people, but to teach them to minister. . . . Truth that is not lived, that is not imparted, loses its life-giving power. . . .

"Many [church members] would be willing to work if they were taught how to begin. . . . Every church should be a training school for Christian workers. . . . Let the teachers lead the way in working among the people, and others, uniting with them, will learn from their example. One example is worth more than many precepts" *(The Ministry of Healing,* pp. 148, 149).

WOULD BE DISCIPLES IF SHOWN HOW
A Gallup poll showed that only 10 percent of all

laypersons were involved in the ministry of the church. Interestingly, 40 percent who are not involved would like to be involved, but they had never been asked to or shown how. Yes, *many* members would become fruit-bearing disciples if they were shown how. LeRoy Eims confirms that "every pastor has in his congregation men who today are merely spectators in the kingdom of God, but who would pay any price to be involved with him in the real heart of the ministry." Then he gives a reason why a pastor may not be willing to grasp such promising opportunity: "But it will cost *him*. Such men need his sermons and instruction, but he will have to share his life with them. And that costs" *(The Lost Art of Disciple Making,* p. 33).

What an immensely vast human resource that has barely been tapped! These are not members who need to be cajoled to be discipled; they are *already* interested and persuaded. What is the problem, then? Why is this precious resource needlessly squandered? Very few disciple-makers live the example of Jesus and model it before them. As Eims said, it is costly. It takes the giving of ourselves to our church members just as Jesus gave Himself to His disciples. He was available to be seen, heard, and touched. They were close to Him and observed Him in their on-the-job training. As they faced the *real* world of pull and push, triumph and trial, peace and peril, commendation and condemnation, He was right there with them to encourage, instruct, and guide.

A LIVING AND LASTING LEGACY

The pastor in our story was a disciple-maker who multiplied himself in his receptive church members. He was not the showy type who paraded himself before others, but he simply modeled Jesus' love and ministry. His greatest joy and fulfillment was to see his trainees mature and become successful fruit-bearing disciples. Some years later a tragic accident took his life. But rich was the legacy the members inherited in continuing to carry on his ministry. For more than a year no pastor was called to that post, yet the trained few continued to reach the many just as their pastor had modeled before them. They proved to be living extensions of their pastor as they continued to preach, teach, counsel, train, witness, model, and prepare others for baptism, just as they did while he was still with them. The experience of that church offered a living demonstration of how Christ modeled and imparted His ministry to His disciples.

Just imagine what would happen if such a dynamic experience would be multiplied in many churches! You see, modeling is where the rubber meets the road. All the previous discussion, important as it is, must lead to application.

TRANSFORMED TO TRANSFORM

This is what Christ's training was about—not merely dispensing good information but investing Himself in modeling His ministry before His disciples. Early in His ministry He told them they were to be "the salt of the earth" and "the light of the world" (Matt. 5:13, 14). But they could never be such on their own. Christ Himself, the salt and the light *par excellence,* was to impress Himself on them in His daily association with them. He was to salt their lives and diffuse His light into their beings so that they could indeed become the salt and the light all around them. Transformed to transform.

Jesus said to them: "And you also will bear witness, because you have been with Me from the beginning" (John 15:27). His valuable information was always intended to lead to their sure transformation. Jesus prayed, showing them how to pray; He taught, showing them how to teach; He healed, showing them how to heal; He evangelized, showing them how to evangelize; He trained, showing them how to train; He made disciples out of them, showing them how to make disciples out of others. What the Master did for them they were to do for others. His most effective training tool was His example, to be emulated and imparted.

JESUS MODELED PRAYER AND SERVICE

You will recall that Jesus modeled His prayer life before His disciples. To Him prayer was never some exercise in displayed piety, but ever the essence of God's power pervading His life. Intimate communion with God refreshed His life, surrounding Him with peace and light. His prayer life resulted in something clearly observable in all His words, actions, and movements. They saw Him totally immersed in conversing with His Father, undistracted by His surroundings.

"He seemed to be in the very *presence* of the Unseen, and there was a *living power* in His words as of one who spoke with God. The hearts of the listening disciples were deeply *moved*. . . . The disciples had come to *connect* His hours of prayer with the power of His words and works. Now, as they listened to His supplication, their hearts were awed and humbled. As He ceased praying, it was with *conviction* of their own deep need that they exclaimed, 'Lord, teach us to pray' (Luke 11:1)" (Ellen G. White, *Thoughts From the Mount of Blessing,* pp. 102, 103; italics supplied).

We see the dynamics of the transforming impact of His modeling on His disciples, don't we? They were moved, they connected His prayer with His power, they were awed and humbled, and with deep conviction they longed to be like Him. He was not like the Pharisees, wanting to parade His prayers in public, but He did not act like a hermit, either. He intended for His disciples to observe Him and learn from Him. He desired them not only to share and participate in His prayer life, but also to be engaged in different aspects of His ministry.

The miracle of feeding the multitude is but one example. Jesus did not want the disciples to send the thousands away hungry, so He commanded them: "You give them something to eat" (Mark 6:37). In Greek the pronoun "you" is emphatic, implying that Christ definitely wanted them to participate fully in this miraculous event. He knew they were prepared to provide the five loaves and two fishes, to organize the multitude and distribute the food, but He also wanted to broaden their vision so that they could think of God's desire to use them miraculously in His service.

TEACHING AND LIVING WHAT HE WAS

Modeling His ministry was certainly an integral part of Christ's mission. Someone has said: "A man teaches what he knows, but lives what he is." Jesus was definitely the Man who taught *what* He knew *and* lived *what* He was. What He taught was precisely who He was. His teaching and living were harmoniously integrated in what He modeled.

Another said: "A father is a man who expects his children to be as good as he meant to be." In other words, parents often discover that they could not live up to their ideals—what they meant to be. That is why children hear a parent say: "Do as I say, not as I do." How thankful we ought to be for Jesus, who lived all that He meant to be and empowers us to live out what He said as well as what He did.

The environment for such authentic modeling was His chosen nucleus of disciples. This environment was conducive for heart-to-heart and mind-to-mind interaction. He did not merely dispense theoretical knowledge to stimulate their minds, but He freely offered Himself in love as the living Model to emulate.

LIFE BEGETS LIFE

"To them, above all others, He gave the advantage of His own companionship. Through personal association He *impressed Himself* upon these chosen colaborers." For "it is only life that begets life" *(Education,* p. 84). We are to receive the impression of Christ's life and ministry in our hearts. "As wax takes the impression of the seal, so the soul is to take the *impression* of the Spirit of God and retain the image of Christ" (Ellen G. White, *Selected Messages,* book 1, p. 337; italics supplied). But how can we copy Christ's lofty example, the One whose excellency is beyond comparison? By His grace and by His Spirit we certainly may, for "He *graciously adapted* His life for universal imitation" (Ellen G. White, *Reflecting Christ,* p. 35; italics supplied).

A SMALL, CLOSE-KNIT GROUP

The disciples were very close to their Master, for they

"had been associated together as members of the family of Jesus" *(Thoughts From the Mount of Blessing,* p. 3). In the atmosphere of a small, close-knit group, meaningful relationships can be formed and real learning and modeling can take place. Encouragement, accountability, exhortation, correction, and evaluation in a closely knit group can lead to mutual spiritual growth and maturity. It is a group small enough to encourage them to participate, yet not too big to lead them to be spectators. It is a group that can help them develop and refine their skills in nurture and outreach, their one-to-one witness or multitude ministry.

In the Western world particularly there is a crucial need for the dynamics of small groups. All around us we see a lack of family nurture and sense of belonging. The breakdown of the family and family ties, the loneliness, the near absence of neighborliness, the ceaseless mobility, the fragmentation of traditional relationships, and the alienation in society all account for the tremendous need for many to have a *family* experience in the church they belong to. If not in the church, then where? To many this is the closest they ever get to having a family. The church needs to be organized in small units in order to fill such a tremendous void for nurture, discipleship, and Christian service. Church members would not feel out of place or lost, but would enjoy being their brothers' and sisters' keepers.

"In our churches let companies be formed for service. . . . The formation of *small companies* as a basis of Christian effort is a plan that has been presented before me *by One who cannot err.* If there is a large number in the church, let the members be formed into small companies, to work not only for the *church members*, but for *unbelievers* also" (Ellen G. White, *Evangelism,* p. 115; italics supplied).

He Transferred His Ministry

Jesus used that intimate small group as a vehicle to model His life and ministry. His passion was to show, model, and transfer His ministry to them. He truly counted on them, entrusting them with His own awesome and sacred mission to the world. "Their office was the most important to which human beings had ever been called, and was second only to that of Christ Himself" *(The Desire of Ages,* p. 291). Jesus had no interest in jealously hoarding His expertise in carrying out His mission, but He generously shared it with them. We are His witnesses, His ambassadors, and He entrusted to us *His* ministry of reconciliation (2 Cor. 5:18-20).

A new church pastor wanted to have the outgoing successful pastor spend some time teaching him. Unfortunately, he was not willing to share or model any of his ideas that helped make his ministry effective. He simply felt his hard-earned ideas were his own and wanted the new pastor to "learn the hard way," as he put it. How vastly different the example of Jesus was! He was willing to model and give away His expertise to help His disciples become truly successful. His first and foremost priority was to save souls, and He wants this priority to be ours as well. He desires us to be like Him, and He wants to share with us the highest human calling that is second only to His. He "was eager and intent upon hiring people He felt could replace Him. 'Greater things than I have done shall you do,' He promised. Jesus kept teaching and sharing and demonstrating it so team members would learn that they, too, had the power to do what He had done" *(Jesus, CEO,* p. 151).

MORE TROUBLE THAN IT IS WORTH?

That is why Jesus so patiently labored with the Twelve in all their ups and downs. He always had the big picture in mind: He needed them to reach the world with the saving message of the gospel. "He takes men as they are, with all their faults and weaknesses, and trains them for His service, if they will be disciplined and taught by Him" *(Education,* p. 91).

"What other reason would Jesus have for such a frustrating experience as trying to work through the Twelve?" Bill Hull asks. "They were self-serving, fearful, ego driven, competitive, forgetful, jealous of one another, slow to learn, even slower to unlearn. Working through this rag-tag bunch must have been like Michael Jordan trying to play basketball in Woody Allen's body. They slowed Jesus down; . . . they were more trouble than most people thought they were worth. Everyone except Jesus, that is" *(The Disciple Making Pastor,* p. 198).

But that is it. That is our problem today. Many Christian leaders feel that reproducing disciples is more trouble than it is worth. They may indeed give tacit approval to modeling ministry as an ideal to be professed occasionally, but not as something practical to be possessed as the heart of their ministry. They say it is more pragmatic to do ministry themselves than to model it and share it with others—easier and more efficient. Well, it may be the easier course to follow, but it most certainly is not more efficient or effective.

Training disciples, no doubt, is a challenging task any way we look at it. And it is more so as it is compounded by the devil's fierce resistance to it. He well knows that this is Christ's chosen strategy to reach the world with His salvation. Therefore, we must tenaciously resist His devious devices, firmly holding on to Christ, who has successfully gone before us. We must endure with patience, knowing that the cause of Christ will *never* be defeated. Our Master knows fully the great challenge we face to implement the strategy of modeling His ministry. He understands. Satan resisted Him, too, on this score. Take courage in these words: "As the world's Redeemer, Christ was constantly confronted with apparent failure. . . . But He would not be discouraged. . . . He knew that truth would finally triumph in the contest with evil" (Ellen G. White, *Gospel Workers,* pp. 514, 515).

THE GREAT NEED FOR POSITIVE ROLE MODELS

Satan has stolen a march on us, creating a deplorable lack in this crucial area of modeling ministry. There is a great need for positive role models in our society today. We are bombarded by seminars on all sorts of topics, and theoretical information abounds everywhere. The entertainment industry lulls many into complacency and vanity, luring them into immorality and violence. Our young people languish for lack of spiritual models to be close to, to observe, and to emulate. A vacuum exists for this that cannot be filled by all the electronic wizardry of our modern age. Children cry out for parents who will lead them by word and deed; students need teachers who will show them how to face life successfully; laypersons await spiritual leaders who will model Christ's ministry and engage them in it.

When we take time to mingle with our people, show God's love, work with them, and win their trust, we discover the above to be true. I have had the privilege on many occasions to help model Christ's way in training our youth in witnessing and other facets of Christian service. The valuable ideas they learned in their schools and churches needed to be put into practice. I would take them with me on Bible studies. They learned about witnessing in the classroom: how to make friends, how to share one's testimony, how to share from the Bible, and how to answer questions. Now they needed practical application.

If the young people were left with all this valuable information but with no viable involvement, it would have led to frustration. It was important for them to know the what, the why, and the how of witnessing, but *now* it was time to *show them how to do it* and to *do it with them*. I would take them along only to observe at the beginning (to their relief), but gradually they would feel more at ease to join in the discussion. This helped build their confidence, especially when people responded to Christ and committed themselves to Him.

In such memorable experiences they knew that the God they had studied about in their Bible classes and Sabbath school was *real*, for they saw Him at work in their witness. On the way back to church or school they would ask questions about what had transpired during the Bible studies. We had the opportunity to evaluate what had happened: affirm what needed affirming, and correct what needed correcting. Investing of themselves in the families we studied with, they felt the need to pray for them and looked forward to seeing them again. Gradually they began giving Bible studies themselves. Many years have passed since. What is heartening about this is that now when I see them they are still active disciples and disciplers in their local churches.

"He who called the fishermen of Galilee is *still* calling men to His service. And He is just *as* willing to manifest His power through us as through the first disciples. *However* imperfect and sinful we may be, the Lord holds out to us the offer of *partnership to Himself, of apprenticeship with Christ.* He invites us to come under the divine instruction, that, *uniting with Christ, we may work the works of Christ"* (*The Desire of Ages,* p. 297; italics supplied).

May God help us wholeheartedly accept His offer of partnership with Himself so that we can be apprentices of the skilled Master, living His life and doing His work.

CHAPTER EIGHT

The MESSENGERS of the Mission

It was not easy to let my 6-year-old daughter ride the small bicycle by herself. It was not a problem explaining to her all about bicycling, showing her how to ride, and even riding our bicycles together. But letting her ride all by herself, seeing her disappear out of my sight, was difficult for me. I was considerably relieved to see her come back home safely from her first brief excursions. Then it was time to "debrief" her about how she applied the instructions given to her. It was time to evaluate, encourage, and correct.

Now at 17 she is preparing to drive the car on her own. And for a father it does not get easier. It is no problem telling her all about the car, showing her how to drive, and even letting her drive when I am sitting next to her. But to let her drive on her own in traffic is another story. Nevertheless, I know that just as I allowed—and even encouraged—her to ride her bicycle by herself, so I will also let her drive the car by herself (no matter how reluctant I may be), because this is the only way for her to become a seasoned driver.

THE RISK AND REWARD OF PRACTICING HIS PLAN

The time had come for Jesus to let His disciples finally

venture out on their own and let them apply, by themselves, the training they had received—what He taught them, showed them, and did with them. That was the best way for them to grow and mature in emulating Christ's example. Modeling His example before them evolved inevitably into sending them out as His trusted messengers. Messengers, by their function, have to leave the locale where they are in order to carry the message of their Master. Of course, Jesus took a risk in sending them out as His trusted representatives. But how else could they learn? How else could He multiply His ministry through them?

Experience is the greatest teacher, because people usually thrive and mature when given responsibility and are then held accountable for it. Yes, there is the opportunity to succeed, yet there is also the risk to fail. But failure is often the gateway to true success. God's kingdom cannot advance unless there is the passing on of the torch of service from leaders to followers and the bequeathing of the legacy of the trainers to the trainees.

That is what Jesus had in mind all along. He pointed to this definite objective at the outset of His ministry. "And He went up on the mountain and called to Him those He Himself wanted. . . . Then He appointed twelve, that they might be with Him and that He might send them out to preach, and to have power to heal sicknesses and to cast out demons" (Mark 3:13-15). It is clear that the objective of being *in* the company of Jesus was for the ultimate purpose of being sent *out* to evangelize the world—train the few to reach the many. Notice the principal points in this text: (1) He Himself called the ones He wanted; (2) He appointed them to be *with Him* so that He might train them to become like Him; (3) Christlikeness will be manifested in being *sent out* to preach, heal sicknesses, cast out demons, and do the works of the Master.

In Mark 6:12, 13 we see the beginning of the fulfillment of this objective. We saw already in Mark 3:13-15 that Jesus called the twelve so that He could *present* His plan to send them out as His messengers. Here He called them to *practice* the plan. They had witnessed their Master preach and heal, and they took part in His ministry. But He was there for them. When they were questioned and harassed, they could always run to Jesus for help and consolation. But in order to multiply Christ's ministry in others they themselves needed to give help to others. However, they could do this only if they were sent out on their own. Jesus was preparing them for the time when He was going to leave.

The timing of Jesus was just right in calling the disciples to venture out on their own. They had listened, observed, and participated sufficiently to at least get started. They had brought people to Jesus, and they had learned to discern and meet their needs, but they were doing all this under the watchful and reassuring eyes of Jesus. Ellen White tells us that "they taught what they had learned of Jesus, and were every day obtaining a rich experience. *But they needed also an experience in laboring alone.* . . . Now, while He was personally with them, to point out their errors, and counsel and correct them, the Saviour sent them forth as *His representatives*" *(The Desire of Ages,* p. 349; italics supplied).

Jesus sent them out by His power to multiply His ministry in their ministry (Mark 6:7-11). It was not easy to leave the security of His presence, but they were assured of His power. In response to His command to go out, "they went out and preached that people should repent. And they cast out many demons, and anointed with oil many who were sick, and healed them" (verses 12, 13).

Robert Coleman uses the apt example of the eagle and its eaglets to illustrate what Jesus needed to do at this juncture of their training. "Like a mother eagle teaching her young to fly by pushing them out of the nest, Jesus pushed His disciples out into the world to try their own wings" (*The Master Plan of Evangelism,* p. 84).

EXPERTISE COMES WITH EXPERIENCE

The young eagles would not fly while enjoying the security of the nest. They must flex their muscles, flutter their wings, and even be shoved out of their "security blanket." And when they are pushed out of the nest, they are not going to be transformed right away into expert flyers like their parents, soaring the lofty heights. Expertise comes with experience; so also with training disciples. Training is a gradual process that is refined through trial and error, through failing and trying again.

This is what Jesus had in mind when He said that "everyone who is perfectly trained will be like his teacher" (Luke 6:40). What does it mean to be perfectly trained? In this text the Greek word translated "perfect" is the perfect passive participle of the verb *katartizō*, which refers in this context to being fully prepared, thoroughly furnished, or fully trained. It was often employed to describe mending something. To become fully trained is obviously not something instantaneous, but something gradual. To emulate our Master in His life and ministry is a daily growing experience.

When the disciples obeyed Christ's command and went out on their *own*, they began the needed process of *owning* their ministry. They found themselves confronted with situations, such as when they were with their Master. And not having Him with them to deal with these situations, they had to handle them themselves. But the Holy Spirit helped them respond as they witnessed Jesus respond in similar circumstances. "When they were separated from Him, every look and tone and word came back to them. Often when in conflict with the enemies of the gospel, they repeated His words, and as they saw their effect upon the people, they rejoiced greatly" *(The Desire of Ages,* p. 350).

Studying Jesus' marching orders to His disciples, as recorded in Matthew 9:36-11:1, is a valuable learning experience for us. His detailed instructions for this third Galilean tour showed how much He cared for the disciples, preparing and warning them about what they were to face on their own. You may recall that the first Galilean tour (Matt. 4:12-17) involved Jesus' preaching of repentance and *announcement* of the establishment of His kingdom of grace. The second Galilean tour commenced after the Sermon on the Mount (Matt. 5-7), when Jesus *demonstrated* the nature of His kingdom. (See also Mark 1:39.)

Now it was time for Him to *deploy* the twelve to advance His kingdom. We find some valuable lessons alluded to in Christ's instructions (Matt. 9:37-11:1) to His disciples as they embarked on their first missionary journey. (Nearly a year later Christ sent out the 70 disciples as His messengers with the same instructions.)

THE MESSENGERS OF THE MISSION

THE MASTER'S MARCHING ORDERS

What are some applications for us—Christ's present-day messengers—entrusted with the crucial task of extending His ministry?

1. Jesus pointed to the desperate need for *spiritual leaders,* leaders who would nurture and guide the weary multitudes scattered like sheep without a shepherd. There were so many who needed His help, those who were oppressed and scattered by unfaithful hirelings. He longed to extend His ministry through faithful undershepherds emulating Him, the Good Shepherd. That is why He said: "The harvest truly is plentiful, but the laborers are few" (Matt. 9:37). The real problem was not with the multitudes, for they were ripe for the harvest. They were ready to be gathered in and become productive members of God's kingdom. The real problem was with the laborers, because there were very few indeed. That was precisely Christ's strategy: faithful laborers, faithful representatives through whom He could extend and multiply His ministry.

Today we are blessed by the incredible technology of cyberspace and satellite transmissions, but that ought never to replace the human contact of Christ's loving laborers. There is a danger that we may become so obsessed with the sophisticated technologies that span even outer space that we may overlook the human space next door to us. Of course, the two can and should complement each other, and when they do they become a giant force to reach the entire world. Nevertheless, Christ always desires to have real human representatives through whom He can touch real people in everyday life. Nothing can ever substitute for being loving disciples whose hearts throb with the loving heart of Jesus. The world all around us is dying for such a loving, living demonstration.

2. Jesus organized His disciples to work *two by two*. Even though He was not going to be with them in person, they were by no means alone, because the Holy Spirit would accompany them, and also a friend or a brother would be at their side. This was the most natural, efficient, and effective way of grouping the disciples. Each one was grouped with someone for mutual support.

"None were sent alone, but brother was associated with brother, friend with friend." And the practical reason for that was so "they could help and encourage each other, counseling and praying together, each one's strength supplementing the other's weakness" *(The Desire of Ages,* p. 350). Disciple-making can become much more successful if Christ's wise counsel is heeded.

It "was the Saviour's purpose that the messengers of the gospel should be associated in this way" *(ibid.).* Solomon, the wise man, attests to this: "Two are better than one, because they have a good reward for their labor. For if they fall, one will lift up his companion. But woe to him who is alone when he falls, for he has no one to help him up" (Eccl. 4:9, 10).

3. Jesus not only assigned each representative a human partner, but more important, He also gave each *divine power and authority*. "And when He had called His twelve disciples to Him, He gave them power" (Matt. 10:1). The Greek word used here is *exousia,* which literally means "authority." Before this the disciples assisted Jesus as He exercised God's authority to preach and to heal, but now they themselves were given His authority over the enemy, authority to preach and heal. What a Master Equipper Jesus is! He made sure they had human support as well as divine power and authority.

However, divine power is what is crucial in extending Christ's ministry. The best that human helpers can offer is to point us to our ultimate Source of power. For without divine power permeating our ministry, all our human camaraderie and training will be of no avail. Others must see that all we do should manifest divine power and be sealed with the stamp of divine authority.

"I just happen to be in this area . . ." was what a pastor I knew would say when making home visitations. This still bothers me whenever I hear it. We, Christ's messengers, endowed with divine power and authority, do not minister to others haphazardly. We are on a divine appointment, engaged in a divine mission that is guided by God's providence to accomplish His specific purpose. Imagine what great impact our ministry would have if we made room for God to exude His power and exercise His authority through us!

4. Jesus sent His disciples first of all to their *immediate areas of influence*. "Do not go into the way of the Gentiles, and do not enter a city of the Samaritans," He commanded them. "But go rather to the lost sheep of the house of Israel" (Matt. 10:5, 6). Why wasn't He more inclusive? Wasn't He interested in the salvation of others as well? Why be so nationalistic in focusing on the lost sheep of Israel and not on the lost sheep of the Gentiles?

The rationale for Jesus' command was by no means an indication of His lack of interest in the Gentiles. To the contrary, it revealed His abundant love for them. Again we see

His disciple-making philosophy at work: equip the few to reach the many. He hoped that through His disciples' witness to the Jews, many of them would in turn become laborers in the vast fields of the Gentiles. In other words, He intended to evangelize the Gentiles by evangelizing the Jews. "If the Jews would receive the gospel, God purposed to make them His messengers to the Gentiles. Therefore they were first to hear the message" *(The Desire of Ages,* p. 351).

Moreover, if Jesus had sent His disciples to the Gentiles and Samaritans first, it would have stirred the prejudice of the Jews needlessly and undermined their effectiveness in working with the Gentiles later. Even the disciples themselves were not prepared to go to the Gentiles on their first missionary venture. Unfortunately they still shared prejudice with all the Jews toward their neighbors, and such prejudice would have certainly thwarted their witness.

It was a matter of divine timing for the disciples as well as for the Jews and non-Jews. Nearly a year later Jesus commissioned the 70 other disciples to go to all the cities, including the Gentile and Samaritan ones. (See Luke 10:1.) The commissioning of the seventy, who followed Jesus and learned from Him, gives us another indication about Jesus' strategy: He was always expanding His force of messengers in ever-widening circles of ministry—the twelve, the seventy, the lost sheep of the house of Israel, the lost sheep of the Samaritans and Gentiles.

We must not bypass the people close to us in order to reach the ones far from us. Our circle of influence must start where we are, and continue to expand in ever wider circles from there. It is tragic when we ignore our immediate sphere of influence—the family, the church, the workplace, the community where we live—in our rush to distant spheres. On our way there we must minister to those along the way. And if we minister well here and now, we will be better equipped and our ministry more credible there and then.

"We need not go to heathen lands, or even leave the narrow circle of the home, if it is there that our duty lies, in order to work for Christ. We can do this in the home circle, in the church, among those with whom we associate, and with whom we do business. The greater part of our Saviour's life on earth was spent in patient toil in the carpenter's shop at Nazareth. . . . He was as faithfully fulfilling His mission while working at His humble trade as when He healed the sick. . . . So, in the humblest duties and lowliest positions of life, we may walk and work with Jesus" (Ellen G. White, *Steps to Christ,* pp. 81, 82).

5. Jesus instructed them to be "*wise* as serpents and *harmless* as doves" (Matt. 10:16). He wanted them to be realists as they faced the "wolves" of the world, yet He wanted them to maintain their idealism. To be harmless and peaceful and loving, yes, but also to balance that out with keeping their eyes of discernment and wisdom wide open.

More than ever before in the history of the world, the messengers of Christ are to exhibit this balance in their ministry: truth spoken in love, firmness mingled with kindness, and prudence infused with peace. They must experience security in their Master as they confront rejection, betrayal, hatred, and even death for His sake. They must be totally dependent on Him in all things, because His Spirit will guide them, speak through them, and help them be faithful to the end.

6. Jesus *practiced what He preached*. "Now it came to pass, when Jesus finished commanding His twelve disciples, that He departed from there to *preach and teach in their cities*" (Matt. 11:1). Leaving the disciples, He Himself immediately embarked on doing exactly what He commanded them to do. He wanted to go on His own so that they might have the incentive and courage to go on their own. He did not remain idle when He sent them on their own, but was engaged in the same ministry He had entrusted to them.

I remember a pastor who inspired, trained, and mobilized us to reach out to our neighbors with our witness. But whenever the time would come to go out, unfortunately, he would always stay behind in the church, promising to pray for us. It always bothered me why he was not willing to do what he had asked us to do. I ached to tell him that he could still pray for us while doing what he asked us to do, but could not. Jesus built up His disciples' morale by doing what He had asked them to do. As their Leader He never asked them to do what He Himself was not willing to do.

COUNTING COST AND CONSIDERING CONSEQUENCES

This was the first time the disciples were about such a mission on their own. Jesus now was not looking over their shoulders, but taking the essential risk that some mistakes would be made. However, they were to return to Him for debriefing, evaluation, and affirmation. He gradually increased their responsibility all along the way while they were with Him. But now the great challenge was this transitional phase from His doing ministry with them to letting them do it themselves. And even though they were not with their Master, as they were being sent out on their own this time, they were still tied to Him, but on a long leash.

I worked as a house painter for a few years to help finance my education. Learning to skillfully use the brush did not come easily or naturally. I had casually watched painters using their brushes many times before, but now I watched them much more carefully, knowing that the brush would be passed on to me. And when that happened, I still made mistakes—despite all my close observation—before gradually becoming a skilled house painter. While I was an apprentice, the skilled house painter was observing my work and offering helpful suggestions as we worked side by side. Later he sent me on a few jobs to paint on my own. He would drop by now and then and evaluate my work. Eventually he stopped coming by because he could now trust my skills to do satisfactory work.

It is clear from Jesus' specific instructions to His disciples that He wanted them to *count the cost of discipleship.* Our skills are refined through failure even at something we have already been successful at. Such failures can become great blessings in disguise when they lead us to sense our need for Christ. We can always go to Him, for He is always there to teach us valuable lessons from our experience. And as we learn from Him, He turns our temporary failures to enduring successes.

The incident of the disciples' failure in Mark 9:14-29 (see also Matt. 17:14-21) is a case in point. After their report of great success in preaching and healing (including casting out demons), recorded in Mark 6:12, 13, we now read of this dismal failure of not being able to cast out the evil spirit from the young man. They were publicly embarrassed and confused as to what they had done wrong this time. Amid this confusion Jesus came to the rescue. He came to heal this youngster, using the incident to further refine His disciples' ministry.

In response to their question as to why they could not heal the child, Jesus pointed out that the problem was with their lack of faith and a prayer life. "Their unbelief, that shut them out from deeper sympathy with Christ, and the carelessness with which they regarded the sacred work committed to them, had caused their failure in conflict with powers of darkness. . . . Instead of strengthening their faith by prayer and meditation on the words of Christ, they had been dwelling on their discouragements and personal grievances" (*The Desire of Ages,* pp. 430, 431).

When given responsibility and held accountable for their actions, their faith grew, their gifts blossomed, and their skills were fine-tuned. They were to learn the valuable lesson of humility in success and teachableness in failure. Sometimes success can lead to failure, and failure can be the impetus for success. And Jesus was there to help them in their ups and downs and to guide them in this growth process of becoming messengers of His mission. He was still there to help them master the mission and to deploy them to take His place when He would leave this earth.

Jesus had great hopes for them as they were to carry out His mission. "He knew that the life of His trusting disciples would be like His, a series of uninterrupted victories, not seen to be much here, but recognized as such in the great hereafter. . . . They are to live as He lived, and work as He worked, because they depend on Him as the great Master Worker. . . . Though apparent impossibilities obstruct their way, by His grace they are to go forward. Instead of deploring difficulties, they are called upon to surmount them. They are to despair of nothing, and to hope for everything" *(ibid.,* p. 679).

CHAPTER NINE

The MASTERING of the Mission

I remember as a youngster my father taking me to our farm to help him graft olive branches into olive trees. We would carefully make an incision in a tree and insert a branch snugly. Covering the incision with mud, we would wrap it tightly and hope the branch would take hold, blossom, and become fruitful. Some time later we would go to see how the grafted branches were doing.

One incident made an unforgettable impression on me. All the grafted branches budded with new leaves except one. When I asked what had happened, Father told me to peel away the wrappings on the grafted area. Then I discovered that the branch never took hold in the tree, and without the connection the branch dried up. The other branches that had become one with the tree were thriving and growing and eventually became fruit-bearing.

Like branches grafted in the vine, the disciples were gradually learning from their Master to master the mission. They were connected to Him and were to remain in Him through the ministry of the promised Holy Spirit. Jesus had prepared them the best way He possibly could. Finally the time was ripe to deploy them and to entrust them to the

Spirit. "Engraft the leafless twig upon the flourishing vine stock, and it becomes a living branch, drawing sap and nourishment from the vine. Fiber by fiber, vein by vein, the sapling clings, until it buds and blossoms and bears fruit" (Ellen G. White, *Sons and Daughters of God,* p. 291).

ENTRUSTED TO THE HOLY SPIRIT

Chapters 14 to 17 of John are crucial to this final phase of Christ's deploying His disciples. He introduces (John 14) and He concludes (John 16) His description of a fruit-bearing disciple (John 15) with the vital role that the Holy Spirit would play. He was preparing to leave them in the Spirit's trusted hands. Yes, they would remain in Him, but in a different way: He would abide with them through His Representative, the Holy Spirit. Their deployment was to be imbued by the Spirit from beginning to end.

In John 14 He assured them that He would not leave them orphans, but would send them the Helper to remind them of all the things He had taught them. Also, the Spirit would teach them everything they needed to know (see verses 16-18, 26). In going to the Father, Jesus was to deploy His disciples to do His works and even greater works than those that He accomplished. He had taught and trained them well, and now He was raising their sights and expectations higher than ever, exceeding anything they had ever seen (see verse 12).

In John 15 Jesus tells them about the dynamics of fruit-bearing discipleship. Such would be actualized in their lives through the enabling power of the Holy Spirit, who always testifies of Jesus (see verse 26).

Characteristics of Fruitful Disciples

According to Jesus, the Master Disciple-maker, what are the distinctive characteristics of fruitful, deployable disciples?

1. They abide in Christ (John 15:7): "If you abide in Me, and My words abide in you, you will ask what you desire, and it shall be done for you." Abiding in Christ depends on our continuous choice to remain in Him. Mature disciples commit themselves daily to a living connection with the Vine through feeding on His Word and living a life of prayer and witness. Such a life cannot be drawn from other branches, but only from the Vine. "One branch is not to borrow its sustenance from another. Our life must come from the parent vine. It is only by personal union with Christ, by communion with Him daily, hourly, that we can bear the fruits of the Holy Spirit" *(Testimonies for the Church,* vol. 5, pp. 47, 48).

2. They bear fruit (verse 5): "He who abides in Me, and I in him, bears much fruit; for without Me you can do nothing." Christ's primary emphasis is not on bearing fruit, but on remaining in Him. Bearing fruit naturally results from adhering to Him. In fact, focusing on the fruit pulls us away from focusing on Him. It is by beholding Him, not the fruit, that we become like Him in His life and ministry. The energizing life of Christ surges through our being, because "as long as the soul reaches toward Christ, there is little danger that he will wilt, and droop, and decay" *(Sons and Daughters of God,* p. 288).

3. They glorify God (verse 8): "By this My Father is glorified, that you bear much fruit." Bearing fruit provides undeniable witness that they have a daily connection to Christ. They possess what they profess, thus authenticating their witness through the power and to the glory of God. By their fruits we shall know whether they are genuine disciples of Christ, for "the same fruit appears upon the branch that is seen upon the tree" *(Sons and Daughters of God, p. 287).*

4. They abide in His love (verse 9): "As the Father has loved Me, I also have loved you; abide in My love." Abiding in Christ results from abiding in His love. His love to them and their love to Him must always be the sole impetus for their continuous connection with Him. Their fruitfulness for Him proceeds from their devotion to Him.

5. They obey Him (verses 10, 14): "If you keep My commandments, you will abide in My love" (verse 10). Jesus teaches that love and obedience go hand in hand. A growing, loving relationship to Christ is maintained by their loving obedience to Him, regardless of the cost. They demonstrate their love to Him by their obedience to Him. They become totally dependable to carry out their Master's will, regardless of their shifty feelings and varying circumstances.

6. They are His friends (verses 14, 15): "No longer do I call you servants, for a servant does not know what his master is doing; but I have called you friends, for all things that I heard from My Father I have made known to you" (verse 15). Christ is not only their Master but also their Friend. This points to their intimate, loving, and obedient relationship with Him. In entrusting them with His mission of making disciples, He opened His heart wide to them, revealing the secrets of reaching the world with His saving gospel. They were always to be His faithful friends and trusted partners, engaged together in a common mission. They were to be guided by His wise leadership and energized by His loving friendship in the thick and thin of their spiritual conquests.

7. They have full joy (verse 11): "These things I have spoken to you, that My joy may remain in you, and that your joy may be full." The acid test of Christ's true disciples is their undiminished inner joy that wells from within despite difficult circumstances. Sharing in Christ's work of making disciples springs forth from a spirit of joy that is anchored in Christ's joy and that results from loving obedience to Him. And His joy flows through their lives until it becomes a mighty current of full joy covering all in its path. For such joy set before them they endure all things to expand Christ's kingdom. Happiness is external, it comes and goes; His joy is within the soul and abides forever. Happiness can always be taken away, but no one can take away the joy of the Lord (see John 16:22).

8. They possess His love (verses 12-14, 17): "This is My commandment, that you love one another as I have loved you" (verse 12). This is the crowning result of all the previously mentioned characteristics: Loving others as Christ loves. That is how the world would know that they were His true disciples. Love must permeate all aspects of their ministry, because it is true that the "strongest argument in favor of the gospel is a loving and lovable Christian" *(The Ministry of Healing,* p. 470).

Loving others with Christlike love is the sure fulfillment of God's law and the genuine expression of His character. The more closely they are united in love with Christ, the more closely they are united in love with each other. But this loving union must be established first with

Christ in order for us to experience a bond of loving unity with one another. "The powers of darkness stand a poor chance against believers who love one another as Christ has loved them" *(Sons and Daughters of God,* p. 286).

The Advantage of Having the Holy Spirit

In John 16 Jesus goes back to the role of the Holy Spirit as He concludes His remarks about the characteristics of fruitful disciples. He expected them to take more initiative and shoulder more responsibility in mastering His mission. They could go only so far with Him around them, but the Spirit would propel them into new heights and drive them into greater exploits. He would keep in contact with them through the Spirit, and the only thing they would lack would be His physical presence. For example, the time comes when a young teacher must be left in the classroom by himself or herself without the supervisor hovering about.

"To all these the disciples were to go as His representatives. The believers would thus be led to look upon them as divinely appointed teachers, and when the Saviour should be taken from them they would not be left without instructors" *(The Desire of Ages,* p. 351). The disciples were now to have more freedom to go forth everywhere with greater responsibility. They were to launch new evangelistic thrusts nearby and far away. They were to train and equip new disciples and penetrate new target areas covering the face of the earth.

That is why Jesus explained to His saddened disciples: "It is to your advantage that I go away; for if I do not go away, the Helper will not come to you; but if I depart, I will send Him to you" (John 16:7). The primary responsibility for the disciples' mastering the mission and for their deployment would now belong to the Holy Spirit.

Here are some of the advantages of the ministry of the Spirit in their deployment:

1. He would be Christ's ever-present *representative with them.* Circumstances might separate them from their loved ones and friends, but nothing could separate them from the Holy Spirit. "And I pray the Father, and He will give you another Helper," Jesus promised, "that He may abide with you *forever*" (John 14:16).

2. He would be present with them in full force, always and everywhere, *to reach the world through them.* He would empower them to the full extent to accomplish even greater works than the works of their Master. Not of greater quality, to be sure, but of greater quantity.

3. He would empower them *to accomplish the grand goal that Christ set before them at the beginning.* "But you shall receive power when the Holy Spirit has come upon you," Jesus promised them, "and you shall be witnesses to Me in Jerusalem, and in all Judea and Samaria, and to the end of the earth" (Acts 1:8).

It is quite significant that Jesus chose this empowering statement to be His *final words* to His disciples. Challenging them to raise their sights to this great task, He *launched* them into discipleship training with these words: "Behold, I say to you, lift up your eyes and look at the fields, for they are already white for harvest!" (John 4:35). Now they were ready to receive the power of the Holy Spirit to harvest the fields and make disciples.

4. Jesus came into this world veiling His divinity in humanity. But the Holy Spirit would come in the fullness

of divine power. "Sin could be resisted and overcome only through the mighty agency of the Third Person of the Godhead, who would come with *no modified energy, but in the fullness of divine power.* It is the Spirit that makes effectual what has been wrought out by the world's Redeemer" *(The Desire of Ages,* p. 671; italics supplied).

5. As they would move in faith to make disciples, **the Spirit Himself would do the convicting of people's hearts.** He would "convict the world of sin, and of righteousness, and of judgment" (John 16:8).

6. The Holy Spirit would **teach them all things,** *and bring to their remembrance all that Christ had taught them (John 14:26).*

7. The Holy Spirit would **guide them into all truth,** *and would tell them "things to come" (John 16:13).* Jesus greatly desired to tell them many things on His heart, but they were not prepared to bear them while He was still with them (verse 12). But now the Spirit was to tell them what Jesus wanted to tell them all along. Jesus "had left unsaid many things that could not be comprehended by the disciples. These also would be opened to them by the Spirit. The Spirit was to quicken their understanding, that they might have an appreciation of heavenly things" *(The Desire of Ages,* pp. 670, 671).

8. The Holy Spirit would **speak in Christ's authority and glorify Him** *before them and the world, for He would take what is Christ's and declare it to them (John 16:13, 14).*

Being With Jesus, Becoming Like Jesus

Luke 6:40 found fulfillment in John 15 and Acts 4:13. In Luke 6:40 there was the promise that *they would become like their Master* as they submitted themselves to His training. And throughout His tenure with them He was helping them become more and more like Him in life and ministry. As we have seen, in John 15, toward the end of their training *they were becoming like Him.* In Acts 4:13 they were fully deployed and empowered by the Holy Spirit, and they were recognized as *having been with Jesus because now they were like Jesus.* They were like branches becoming one with the Vine—sturdy branches that were no longer tossed back and forth and blown in every direction, but anchored securely in the Vine.

Christ's life was flowing through them, and the Spirit's power was energizing them to produce and reproduce the goodly fruits of their Master. Notice how *being* with Christ had resulted in *becoming* like Christ: "When the disciples came forth from the Saviour's training, they were no longer ignorant and uneducated. *They had become like Him* in mind and character, and men took knowledge of them that *they had been with Jesus*" *(The Desire of Ages,* p. 250; italics supplied).

Becoming like Christ in mind and character actuated all their work for Him. They might teach all the doctrines He taught them eloquently, but unless they possessed His love, they were not truly representing Him. Not to possess a character like Christ's would deny whatever they would profess. But as they became sanctified by His truth, their powerful profession of His name was a genuine expression of their possession of Christlikeness. They were ready now to be deployed and sent into the world just as the Father sent His Son into this world. Jesus said: "As You sent Me into the world, I also have sent them into the world" (John 17:18). Now they were prepared to reproduce the life and ministry of their Master in their lives and the lives of many others. Jesus' giving His ministry away to His disciples is evidenced in what He commissioned Peter to do just before His ascension (John 21:15-19). Three things are evident in the deployment of Peter.

1. Supreme love for Jesus. Supreme love for Jesus is at the core of lasting loyalty to His mission. That is why at the very close of His ministry He raised this issue with Peter three times. Two times Jesus asked Peter whether He loved Him. One time He asked him whether He loved Him more than the other disciples. Such deep love and staunch loyalty to the Master must be the hallmark of His deployable disciples. That is what would sustain them to face severe trials, to brave the heat of battle, and to remain faithful even unto death.

2. Feeding His sheep. Following Peter's heartfelt declaration of His love, three times Jesus also commanded him to feed His flock. Love for Christ must always manifest itself in doing His work of nurturing and equipping His people to be productive. These were Christ's own precious sheep whom He entrusted to His faithful disciple in order to help them grow strong, reproduce, and multiply themselves.

3. Faithful even unto death. A disciple who loves His Master supremely and faithfully tends His flock and is ready to give up life itself for Him. Christ can accomplish great feats through disciples who do not count their lives dear and who are ready to lay down their lives for the cause. Such discipleship can be a very costly business. It can lead to sacrificing their lives for the sake of the gospel as Christ did. Jesus spoke prophetically when He said of Peter: " 'But when you are old, you will stretch out your hands, and another will gird you and carry you where you do not wish.' This He spoke, signifying by what death he would glorify God" (verses 18, 19).

TO PERSEVERE IS TO PREVAIL

The disciples were now in the hands of the Holy Spirit, poised to be fired by His Pentecostal outpouring and prepared to turn the world upside down for the cause of Christ. Through the Spirit's power they were now poised to launch the movement of the mission of reproducing and multiplying disciples in all the world.

As was their Master, they would be confronted with great obstacles, but they would not be discouraged. Jesus knew that His "bloodstained banner would wave triumphantly over His followers. He knew that the life of His trusting disciples would be like His, a series of uninterrupted victories, not seen to be such here, but recognized as such in the great hereafter" *(The Desire of Ages,* p. 679).

This is where spiritual perseverance counts. To persevere is to prevail. To be tenacious is to triumph. With absolute confidence that we have a winner on our side, we move forward with undaunted courage in Jesus' mighty name and in the might of His Spirit.

I once saw a poster showing a frightened cat hanging on to a branch with the caption beneath: "Hang in there, baby!" Spiritual tenacity is born out of a soul conviction about the absolute righteousness and the ultimate triumph of the cause of Christ. According to Oswald Chambers perseverance is more than endurance—it is endurance combined with absolute assurance and certainty that what we are looking for is going to happen. Perseverance means more than just hanging on (which may be only exposing our fear of letting go and falling). It is our supreme effort of refusing to believe that our hero (Jesus) is going to be conquered (see *My Utmost for His Highest,* Feb. 22).

BELIEVING IS SEEING

We are often caught up in what is immediate and seen. We find ourselves struggling with living by sight and not by faith. But as mature disciples of Christ, we must learn from Him to take the long look, to dwell on what is of eternal, not temporal, consequences. We must finally learn that what is unseen is more real than what is seen. As fruit-bearing disciples we must live by faith and not by sight. The motto of our radical discipleship is "Believing is seeing."

Our Master, while empowering us to live His radical discipleship, is also empathizing with the challenges such discipleship confronts us with. That should give us constant courage. "As the world's Redeemer, Christ was *constantly* confronted with *apparent failure.* He seemed to do little of the work which He longed to do in uplifting and saving. . . . But He would *not be discouraged.* . . . He knew that truth would *finally triumph* in the contest with evil" *(Gospel Workers,* pp. 514, 515; italics supplied).

Christ is the Master and the Mover of His mission of making disciples. Persevering with Him is what helps us in mastering this mission and moving it to regions beyond.

CHAPTER TEN

The MOVEMENT of the Mission

A year ago a gardener friend gave me a few cuts from his mint plants. He assured me that they would have no problem growing in our garden. And grow they surely did! They not only grew, but they also thrived. They reproduced and multiplied all over the place. New roots and shoots were perpetually expanding so that in time they took over our entire garden. In a similar way, Christ's few disciples reproduced and multiplied themselves into an ever-expanding movement, moving His mission forward into their entire world.

REPRODUCTION AND MULTIPLICATION

Reproduction is essential to multiplication, but different from it. Disciples may reproduce themselves in new disciples, but unless these new disciples reproduce themselves in turn, there would be no multiplication. Consequently, this dynamic process becomes short-circuited. That is what Jesus was alluding to when He told His disciples that their fruit should not be temporary, but enduring (John 15:16). This reproduction leads to the multiplication that will endure in its ever-expanding forward movement.

One day while I was visiting with an elderly woman, she proudly told me that she had 32 great-grandchildren, 12 grandchildren, and five children. Here we truly have a powerful demonstration of reproduction and multiplication. Of course, there would have been no family multiplication and enlargement had not the children and the grandchildren reproduced. Multiplication continues to occur when reproduction is perpetual. Without such a perpetual process there would be stagnation, weakness, and eventual death.

That is the reason Jesus phrased His last marching orders the way He did. He commissioned His disciples to make disciples. According to Bill Hull, " 'make *disciples* of all nations,' means much more than 'make *converts* of all nations.' Only healthy disciples reproduce. If the church fails to make disciples, it fails to multiply. If the church fails to multiply, it fails" *(The Disciple Making Pastor,* p. 132; italics supplied). It seems that most of the church's resources are depleted on maintaining itself at worst, and making new church members at best, but not on making fruit-bearing disciples.

CHRIST DEMANDS A GREAT DEAL

Hull goes on to state that a major cause for the rarity of multiplication of disciples is "the unwillingness of the church to make disciples." Then he explains the reason for such reluctance: "It takes too long and calls for major restructuring of existing churches. It's much easier to maintain the status quo. Everyone experiences the powerful temptation to cave in to conventional measurements for success. Bodies, bucks, and buildings are the contemporary standards for having the 'right stuff.'" But this means "nothing more than having 'the right fluff,'" which makes many churches seem healthy on the surface, "but in reality, they are factories that produce weakness. If you demand little and put on a good show, you can always get a crowd" *(ibid.,* p. 134).

But Christ demands a great deal. He does not demand a great outward show, but a genuine transformation of our inner self by His Spirit. He demands nothing less than the total giving of self in faithful obedience to the Great Commission. The fulfilling of Christ's Great Commission to make disciples is the very heartbeat of the church, and without it paralysis, decay, and death ensue. We are to broaden our horizons and move the mission of making disciples forward to the unreached millions around the world. "Alas, how many are toiling to fan the spark of life in a church that is ready to die! How many churches are tended like sick lambs by those who ought to be seeking for the lost sheep! And all the time millions upon millions without Christ are perishing" *(The Desire of Ages,* p. 825).

Let us always remember that Christ's Great Commission was not to *become* disciples, but to *make* disciples. We must then be engaged in the business of not merely getting converts, but in equipping disciples to make other disciples—to become active workers in reproducing and multiplying themselves in others. Where the rubber meets the road, disciples are not truly disciples of Christ unless they are disciple-makers for Christ.

I would much rather place $1,000 in an investment or a business venture, in which the money can "reproduce" and "multiply" itself, than to have $10,000 carefully counted, added up, and safely tucked away. In the long run the smaller amount is a greater amount in every way. Likewise with church members. I would rather have one worker disciple whose passion is to reproduce and multiply himself or herself in others than to have 10 pew-warming members who keep coming, but never compound. The living church of Christ must be engaged in the business of ever moving His mission forward through His fruit-bearing disciples.

FORWARD MOMENTUM

Every chapter in this book has been gradually leading to moving this monumental mission forward. In the training of Christ's disciples, the momentum had been building all along, compressing it into the Great Commission and propelling it into the movement. And in its forward movement it advanced in its spiritual realm, proliferated in its geographical reach, multiplied in the numerical domain, and exploded into massive reproduction and multiplication. Indeed, Christ's disciples and the fruit-bearing disciples they reproduced and multiplied turned the world upside down.

Notice how this movement was propelled forward in its various spheres seen in the beginning of the book of Acts.

1. Movement in spiritual advancement. At the day of Pentecost the disciples were all found "with one accord," and "they were all filled with the Holy Spirit" (Acts 2:1, 4). The envious and quarreling disciples were now united in the Spirit. This spiritual maturing can happen only through the working of the Holy Spirit. The message of Peter was so infused with spiritual power that his listeners "were cut to the heart" (verse 37). Such arresting conviction of the human heart is stirred only by the Spirit. And it was only through the energizing of the Spirit that their labor was fruitful (verses 41, 47).

The same holds true for the boldness of the disciples. Just a few weeks earlier they were little more than cowards cringing in fear, but now they were courageous conquerors (Acts 4:13). Peter, intimidated by a servant into denying his Lord three times, now boldly informs the Sanhedrin that he would rather obey God than man (verses 19, 20). The once-fearful disciple now stood firm and stared fear in the face. His faith did not flinch.

As you recall, Jesus promised His disciples early on that as a result of His training they would become like Him (Luke 6:40). Now we see how they had progressed in their spiritual advancement, for even their enemies had to recognize that "they had been with Jesus" because they were acting like Jesus (Acts 4:13). People naturally desire recognition for becoming great or having a high position. But the Spirit's supernatural transformation leads us to learn that the greatest recognition in this world is the recognition for having been with Christ. And the highest accomplishment in this life is indeed to be like Christ. Advancement in the spiritual sphere is the only impetus for any other advancement moving the mission forward.

2. Movement in geographical proliferation. Christ's Great Commission of making disciples of *all the nations* in Matthew 28:19 is specified and reconfirmed in Acts. The outpouring of the Holy Spirit upon the disciples was to be *followed* by an outpouring of their witness to all the world. "But you shall receive power when the Holy Spirit has come upon you; and you shall be witnesses to Me in

Jerusalem, and in all Judea and Samaria, and to the end of the earth" (Acts 1:8).

The Great Commission means making disciples of all in the world by all in the church. That is how the scope of the mission is enlarged to engulf the entire world. Reaching the world with the gospel calls for the training of all believers in the divine art of spiritual reproduction and multiplication. Reaching unbelievers and training believers are intimately intertwined. "The Saviour's commission to the disciples included *all* the believers. It includes *all* believers in Christ *to the end of time*. It is a *fatal mistake* to suppose that the work of saving souls depends alone on the ordained minister. . . . *All* who receive the life of Christ are ordained to work for the salvation of their fellowmen. For this work the church was established, and all who take upon themselves its sacred vows are thereby pledged to be coworkers with Christ" *(The Desire of Ages,* p. 822; italics supplied).

The vast geographical expansion begins with a ripple effect of ever-widening circles, engulfing the whole world with the gospel. It must be launched where we are and extended into the outer regions. That was Christ's idea when He launched His disciples in Jerusalem first and that small circle kept enlarging into the wider spheres of Judea and Samaria, eventually reaching the ends of the world.

But with all places in the world, why start in Jerusalem? Why not go to a new place and get a fresh start? After all, Jerusalem painfully reminded them of all the terrible things that had caused them so much grief and fear. That is precisely the point: God did not want them to flee from fear, but to face it with faith. Thus from the temporary ashes of an apparent tragedy He could build a solid bulwark of faith and erect an eternal monument to His triumph.

A veteran of the war in Vietnam told me that he felt compelled to go back to the place he experienced "hell on earth" so that he could "exorcize the war demons" haunting him. During his tour he dared to go to where he had been imprisoned and tortured. He listened to the young and old as he moved about and found himself coming to terms with his long nightmare as he mixed and sympathized with the people. Consequently, he was able to turn this hideous nightmare of hating his enemies into a living dream of helping them. This soldier learned valuable lessons he would not have learned any other way.

We need to start in our "Jerusalems" to face our fears and fight the good fight of faith before we flee to other fields of labor. There are valuable lessons to be learned from our labor *here and now* that will give us the needed preparation for our labor *there and then*. Laboring in Jerusalem prepared them for Judea. Their experiences in Judea helped them become more effective in Samaria. And their ministry in Samaria equipped them to reach other parts of the world. "The disciples were to begin their work where they were. The hardest and most unpromising field was not to be passed by. So every one of Christ's workers is to begin where he is. . . . Let us do faithfully the work that is nearest. Then let our efforts be extended as far as God's hand may lead the way" *(The Desire of Ages,* p. 822).

Christ's mission to make disciples of all nations is global in its reach. He came not to save one people or one country, but the world, transcending any boundaries of land, race, culture, or religion. That is why He will not come again until "this gospel of the kingdom will be preached in all the world as a witness to all the nations, and then the end will come" (Matt. 24:14).

3. Movement in numerical multiplication. It is mentioned three times in Acts 2 and 4 that souls were added to the early church. The first time was after the Spirit-filled preaching of Peter, which brought in 3,000 souls. The second time refers to the Lord adding "to the church daily those who were being saved" (Acts 2:47). The third time, 5,000 souls joined the church in the aftermath of persecution (Acts 4:4).

Notice that the increase occurred in the context of three special circumstances: (a) Spirit-filled preaching; (b) Spirit-filled fellowship of study, prayer, praise, worship, and social interaction; (c) persecution for righteousness' sake.

If we are not seeing a movement in numerical multiplication in some of our churches, isn't it because we are not experiencing what the early church experienced in these three crucial areas of preaching, fellowship, and persecution? Isn't it because we are not enjoying a dynamic and essential relationship between inreach and outreach, nurture and evangelism? Of course, numbers are not everything, though they are tangible evidence of life and growth. God can work with one person or with a multitude. And while we think of numerical multiplication, we must also keep in mind that "success does not depend upon numbers. God can deliver by few as well as by many. He is honored not so much by the great numbers as by the character of those who serve Him" (Ellen G. White, *Patriarchs and Prophets,* p. 550). "The humblest worker, moved by the Holy Spirit, will touch invisible chords, whose vibrations will ring to the ends of the earth, and make melody through eternal ages" *(The Desire of Ages,* p. 823).

THE GENIUS OF CHRIST'S WAY

God's ideal for the movement in numerical expansion is quality as well as quantity. But He desires to see quality first, for quality determines quantity. Quality disciples who are fruit-bearing guarantee reproduction and multiplication of fruitful disciples. To reap a healthy harvest we must plant a healthy seed. It is often the case that people treat others as they had been treated. Likewise, it is quite likely that people witness to others as they had been witnessed to, or disciple others as they had been discipled. They must begin right in order to end right. And Christ's way is the right way to make disciples. It guarantees the best quality and the greatest quantity.

The genius of Christ's way is the genius of the forward momentum of perpetual quality reproduction of fruitful disciples resulting in quality multiplication. It feeds on itself and is self-perpetuating. That is the only way which results in the right quantity. Christ's way of making disciples has the awesome potential of reaching the entire world, beginning with fruitful disciples reaching and reproducing other disciples after their kind. Jesus, the Way, longs to see His way find a familiar path to our hearts. This is how He will reproduce, multiply, and move His mission of fruit-bearing disciples in our Jerusalems, Judeas, Samarias, and beyond to engulf our entire world.

BIBLIOGRAPHY

Bonhoeffer, Dietrich. *The Cost of Discipleship*. New York: Macmillan Pub. Co., 1976.

Bounds, E. M. *Power Through Prayer*. Grand Rapids: Zondervan Pub. House. Chambers, Oswald. *My Utmost for His Highest*. Grand Rapids: Discovery House, 1992.

Coleman, Robert E. *The Master Plan of Discipleship*. Old Tappan, N.J.: Fleming H. Revell Co.

———. *The Master Plan of Evangelism*. Old Tappan, N.J.: Fleming H. Revell Co., 1980.

———. *The Mind of the Master*. Old Tappan, N.J.: Fleming H. Revell Co., 1977.

Eims, LeRoy. *The Lost Art of Disciple Making*. Grand Rapids: Zondervan Pub. House, 1978.

Griffiths, Michael. *The Example of Jesus*. Downers Grove, Ill.: InterVarsity Press, 1985.

Harrison, Everett F. *A Short Life of Christ*. Grand Rapids: Eerdmans Publishing, 1968.

Hull, Bill. *The Disciple Making Pastor*. Old Tappan, N.J.: Fleming H. Revell Co., 1988.

———. *Jesus Christ Disciple Maker*. Old Tappan, N.J.: Fleming H. Revell Co., 1984.

Jones, Laurie Beth. *Jesus, CEO*. New York: Hyperion, 1995.

Nichol, Francis D., ed. *The Seventh-day Adventist Bible Commentary*. Washington, D.C.: Review and Herald Pub. Assn., 1980. Vols. 6, 7.

Ortiz, Juan Carlos. *Call to Discipleship*. Plainfield, N.J.: Logos International, 1975.

Samaan, Philip G. *Christ's Way to Spiritual Growth*. Hagerstown, Md.: Review and Herald Pub. Assn., 1995.

————. *Portraits of the Messiah in Zechariah*. Hagerstown, Md.: Review and Herald Pub. Assn., 1989.

Watson, David. *Called and Committed*. Wheaton, Ill.: Harold Shaw Publishers, 1982.

White, Ellen G. *The Acts of the Apostles*. Mountain View, Calif.: Pacific Press Pub. Assn., 1911.

————. *The Desire of Ages*. Mountain View, Calif.: Pacific Press Pub. Assn., 1898.

————. *Education*. Mountain View, Calif.: Pacific Press Pub. Assn., 1903.

————. *Evangelism*. Washington, D.C.: Review and Herald Pub. Assn., 1946.

————. *Gospel Workers*. Washington, D.C.: Review and Herald Pub. Assn., 1915.

————. *The Ministry of Healing*. Mountain View, Calif.: Pacific Press Pub. Assn., 1905.

————. *Patriarchs and Prophets*. Mountain View, Calif.: Pacific Press Pub. Assn., 1890.

————. *Reflecting Christ*. Hagerstown, Md.: Review and Herald Pub. Assn., 1985.

————. *Selected Messages*. Washington, D.C.: Review and Herald Pub. Assn., 1958

————. *Sons and Daughters of God*. Washington, D.C.: Review and Herald Pub. Assn., 1955.

————. *Steps to Christ*. Chicago: Fleming H. Revell, 1892.

————. *Testimonies for the Church*. Mountain View, Calif.:

Pacific Press Pub. Assn., 1948.

————. *Thoughts From the Mount of Blessing*. Washington, D.C.: Review and Herald Pub. Assn., 1956.

Wilkins, Michael J. *Following the Master*. Grand Rapids: Zondervan Pub. House, 1992.

Wilson, Carl. *With Christ in the School of Disciple Building*. Grand Rapids: Zondervan Publishing House, 1976.

CHRIST'S
METHOD ALONE

CHRIST'S WAY OF
RELATIONAL WITNESSING

PHILIP G. SAMAAN

There are many ways that attempt to reach people, but Christ's Method is the only one which gives true success. Combined with God's love and intercessory prayer it cannot fail. The focus is on the fine art of relational witnessing. It presents the six steps of Christ's way of reaching people, and how we may successfully model such steps in all our spheres of influence. The book is punctuated with numerous illustrations and experiences to make it easy to apply.

DARE
TO BE A
DANIEL

Empowering
The Final Remnant

Philip G. Samaan

Numerous books had already been written about Daniel's prophecies, but this book focuses more on Daniel's character as an empowering model for the final remnant. The issues he faced then we are and will be facing in these last days. Issues such as lifestyle, worship, persecution that challenge us to be modern-day Daniels. The words of the familiar chorus aptly puts it this way: "Dare to be a Daniel, dare to stand alone, dare to have a purpose firm, dare to make it known."

May this book, by God's grace, help us to become God's showcases and His bright stars shining in this dark world as we bask in the brilliant rays of the Son of Righteousness.

Abraham's Other Son

ISLAM
AMONG JUDAISM & CHRISTIANITY

PHILIP G. SAMAAN

Q'S & A'S

This book delves into the enduring legacy of Abraham, and the longest-running family feud among his descendants. It answers in a clear and practical way 250 questions that puzzle the Western mind about this crucial subject. It is hoped that the question-and-answer format will make the material easier to understand. The book focuses more on Islam than on Judaism and Christianity simply because we are more familiar with the latter two. May the common ground of understanding replace the battleground of misunderstanding. May this journey help prepare us and all of God's children to meet Jesus—the true Seed of Abraham—when He comes.

CHRIST'S WAY OF AFFIRMATION

EMBRACING ALTRUISTIC AFFIRMATION
ESCAPING FOOLISH FLATTERY

PHILIP G. SAMAAN

There is a vacuum that God created in the human heart for altruistic affirmation; and Jesus shows how to demonstrate that in our spheres of influence—marriage, family, church, and community. However, Satan counterfeits such altruistic affirmation which brings glory to God with false flattery which manipulates and inflates human ego. Let Jesus guide and enable you to follow His example in building people up instead of tearing them down.

CHRIST'S
WAY TO PRAY

HOW CHRIST PRAYS FOR US AND WITH US

PHILIP G. SAMAAN

Do your prayers seem to bounce off the wall and back into your face? Do you feel as if your petitions barely reach the ceiling before falling back shattered at your feet? How can your puny prayers become prevailing prayers?

Christ's Way to Pray explains that the answer is not found in focusing on our own fickle faith or puny prayers, but focusing on Christ's formidable faith and powerful prayers. The real answer is found in joining our weak prayers with Christ's mighty prayers. The Christ who prays for us and with us personally, passionately, powerfully, and perpetually.

Christ longs to take our "smelly" prayers and fragrance them with the "much incense" of His prayers. He yearns to take the trickle of our prayers and mingle it with the mighty flood of His prayers.

As you linger in the embrace of the praying Jesus, let Him encircle you with His compassionate human arm as the Son of Man, and with His sovereign divine arm as the Son of God let Him grasp the throne of the Infinite.